Learning Azure DevOps

Outperform DevOps using Azure Pipelines, Artifacts, Boards, Azure CLI, Test Plans and Repos

Myra Kelnor

GitforGits®
ASIAN PUBLISHING HOUSE

Published by: GitforGits

Publisher: Sonal Dhandre

www.gitforgits.com

support@gitforgits.com

Printed in India

First Printing: August 2024

ISBN: 978-81-19177-31-8

Cover Design by: Kitten Publishing

Prologue

Upon beginning my journey with Azure DevOps, I was astounded by its immense power and versatility. The more I looked into it, the more I realized that it was a full-featured platform with the potential to automate, streamline, and revolutionize our DevOps strategy, rather than merely another toolset. Managing numerous teams, projects, and infrastructure simultaneously is a major challenge in today's cloud workflows, and I learned this firsthand as I worked with Azure DevOps on actual projects. "Learning Azure DevOps," is a reflection of my experiences, and I hope it serves as a useful resource for professionals looking to adopt DevOps at scale.

My intention all along was to provide an opportunity for practical training. As the reader, what I want from you is action, not merely reading. Each chapter is organized around practical tasks that you can complete as you progress. Whether you're building CI/CD pipelines or managing containerized applications, I'll walk you through each step. For example, you'll quickly learn how to create and configure Azure DevOps projects, integrate GitHub repositories, and implement automated workflows. One of the most significant aspects of this book is its emphasis on real-world scenarios. We start with fundamental concepts like integrating your source code repository and using YAML to define pipelines before progressing to more advanced topics like Infrastructure as Code (IaC) with Terraform. Each task builds on the previous one to ensure that you have a consistent learning experience. This isn't just about setting things up and moving on. It's about understanding why we make certain decisions, how they affect the overall DevOps lifecycle, and how to apply these principles in your own work environments.

I wanted to make sure that this book portrayed the importance of collaboration in modern DevOps. From creating shared pipelines to collaborating with multiple teams, I emphasize how to align DevOps practices with teamwork. We'll look at the features of Azure Boards, including how to track work items, bugs, and sprints in a way that is understandable to both developers and project managers. You'll learn how to strike a balance between productivity and transparency, so that everyone on the team is aware of the project's current state at all times.

This book will teach you automate everything from builds and tests to database migrations and infrastructure provisioning. By the end, you'll be able to create an automated pipeline that not only builds and tests your application, but also deploys it to a scalable cloud environment such as Azure Kubernetes Service (AKS), including disaster recovery and backup procedures. These are skills that will change the way you and your team deliver software.

I think this book's pragmatic approach will speak to you as a professional who wants to become an expert in Azure DevOps. This is not about theoretical knowledge; it is about providing you with the tools and confidence to use Azure DevOps effectively in your daily work.

Content

Preface

To help cloud professionals make the most of the Azure DevOps platform, "Learning Azure DevOps" is a practical book that walks them through the process step-by-step. This book goes over all the bases of DevOps, including how to automate crucial tasks, deploy infrastructure as code (IaC), and set up and manage CI/CD pipelines.

At the outset, the chapters will teach readers how to create Azure DevOps projects and link their repositories to VCSes like GitHub. Any application's build, test, and deployment processes, including Spring Boot's, can be automated with Azure Pipelines by configuring Pipeline as Code using YAML. To make sure that professionals can manage scalable, cloud-native apps, we also cover advanced topics like containerizing apps with Docker and deploying them to Azure Kubernetes Service (AKS).

Using frameworks such as JUnit, Mockito, and Postman, the book goes even further into automated testing to guarantee quality assurance and continuous testing. It teaches to automate backup and disaster recovery procedures for resilient operations and to use Flyway to perform schema migrations. Additionally, teams are guided to work efficiently together through Azure Boards, shared pipelines, and centralized infrastructure management, highlighting collaboration. Also covered is Azure DevOps Analytics, which readers can use to keep tabs on their projects and teams' performance using real-time dashboards.

In this book you will learn how to:

- Integrate with Git for version control and set up Azure DevOps projects.
- Develop YAML-based Pipeline as Code to streamline the process of automating builds, tests, and deployments.
- Dockerize your apps and then launch them on AKS.
- Utilize Azure Boards and Project Boards to manage and monitor work items, tasks, and user stories.
- Add Postman, JUnit, and Mockito to your continuous integration pipelines to automate your application testing.
- Integrate Flyway into your Azure Pipelines to automate database schema migrations and achieve continuous delivery.
- Facilitate cross-team and cross-project cooperation by establishing shared pipelines and resources.
- Use Azure DevOps Analytics and performance insights for project management and monitoring.

- Deploy backups and failover procedures automatically in Azure DevOps.
- Use Terraform in conjunction with Azure Pipelines to deploy cloud-based IaC.

GitforGits

Prerequisites

If you're a cloud professional or a devops user looking to automate workflows, streamline development processes, and expertly manage DevOps tasks with Azure DevOps, then this book is for you.

Codes Usage

Are you in need of some helpful code examples to assist you in your programming and documentation? Look no further! Our book offers a wealth of supplemental material, including code examples and exercises.

Not only is this book here to aid you in getting your job done, but you have our permission to use the example code in your programs and documentation. However, please note that if you are reproducing a significant portion of the code, we do require you to contact us for permission.

But don't worry, using several chunks of code from this book in your program or answering a question by citing our book and quoting example code does not require permission. But if you do choose to give credit, an attribution typically includes the title, author, publisher, and ISBN. For example, "Learning Azure DevOps by Myra Kelnor".

If you are unsure whether your intended use of the code examples falls under fair use or the permissions outlined above, please do not hesitate to reach out to us at support@gitforgits.com.

We are happy to assist and clarify any concerns.

Acknowledgement

I owe a tremendous debt of gratitude to GitforGits, for their unflagging enthusiasm and wise counsel throughout the entire process of writing this book. Their knowledge and careful editing helped make sure the piece was useful for people of all reading levels and comprehension skills. In addition, I'd like to thank everyone involved in the publishing process for their efforts in making this book a reality. Their efforts, from copyediting to advertising, made the project what it is today.

Finally, I'd like to express my gratitude to everyone who has shown me unconditional love and encouragement throughout my life. Their support was crucial to the completion of this book. I appreciate your help with this endeavour and your continued interest in my career.

Chapter 1: Getting Started with Azure DevOps

Overview

Azure DevOps is an all-inclusive platform for managing and automating the development lifecycle; in this chapter, we will handson the basics needed to start working with it. You will begin by learning the fundamentals of Azure DevOps, including its various services such as Azure Pipelines, Azure Repos, and Azure Boards. Services like these make it easier for teams to work together, automate builds, and release apps more quickly. The goal is to highlight to you how Azure DevOps can help your development and operations teams work together more effectively by providing a single platform for all your modern DevOps practices.

Next, we will walk you through the process of creating an Azure DevOps organization and projects. This will include setting up your account and organization to manage repositories, pipelines, and testing environments. You will also learn how to organize multiple projects into a single organization for effective collaboration and workflow management. The emphasis will be on practical implementation, allowing you to lay a solid foundation for the projects that will be developed throughout this book. We will then walk you through the installation and configuration of Azure CLI to interact with Azure services directly from the terminal.

Finally, you will see how to clone and configure the Spring Boot REST API sample application in Visual Studio Code. This includes importing the project, managing dependencies, and configuring it using Azure DevOps.

What is Azure DevOps?

Azure DevOps is a comprehensive set of tools and services from Microsoft designed to support teams in planning, developing, delivering, and managing software efficiently. It integrates development (Dev) and operations (Ops) into a single workflow, enabling continuous integration, continuous delivery, version control, project management, and testing. One of its most significant advantages is the ability to use it as a cloud-based service that can be scaled and adapted to both small teams and large enterprises. Azure DevOps provides a seamless environment for deploying projects across various platforms and technologies, making it versatile for any modern development team.

One of the primary advantages of Azure DevOps is its flexibility. Teams can use the full set of Azure DevOps services, or they can integrate individual services with their existing toolchains. For example, if a team is already using GitHub for version control, they can still leverage Azure Pipelines for CI/CD. The system is designed to adapt to the specific needs of the organization, allowing them to work with existing tools or replace them with Azure's offerings.

Another key advantage is its robust support for automation and scalability. Azure DevOps allows you to automate virtually every aspect of the software lifecycle, from code integration to deployment. This reduces manual errors and allows teams to focus on building new features instead of managing complex infrastructure. Scalability is another significant benefit, as Azure

DevOps can handle projects of any size. Whether you are a small startup or a large enterprise, it provides the tools necessary to manage everything from a small codebase to large, distributed systems.

Services Offered by Azure DevOps

Azure DevOps offers a suite of services that cater to various aspects of the software development lifecycle. These services, when used together, form a unified platform that simplifies the adoption of DevOps practices across teams. Each service is built to work both independently and in concert with other Azure DevOps services.

Azure Repos

Azure Repos provides Git repositories or Team Foundation Version Control (TFVC) to manage your source code. It supports collaboration through pull requests, code reviews, and branches, enabling teams to manage their codebase effectively. Azure Repos is built with deep integration into other Azure services, making it easy to connect your code to pipelines, testing tools, and deployments.

One key advantage of Azure Repos is its built-in security and compliance features. It offers role-based access controls, ensuring only authorized users have access to specific parts of the codebase. This is particularly useful in enterprise environments where compliance and data security are essential. The integration with Git also means you can use common version control workflows, such as branching and merging, to manage code in a distributed team.

Azure Pipelines

Azure Pipelines is a continuous integration and continuous delivery (CI/CD) service that allows you to build, test, and deploy code automatically. It supports multiple languages and platforms, including .NET, Java, Node.js, Python, and more. Whether you are deploying to Kubernetes, virtual machines, or App Services, Azure Pipelines helps automate the entire deployment process, ensuring that code can be delivered more quickly and reliably.

One of the notable features of Azure Pipelines is its multi-stage pipelines, which allow you to define workflows that involve several environments, such as development, staging, and production. You can configure gates, approvals, and automated tests at each stage, ensuring your application is thoroughly tested and vetted before it reaches users. This is invaluable for enterprises that need robust deployment workflows across multiple regions or customer environments.

Azure Pipelines also integrates with various tools, including GitHub, Bitbucket, and GitLab. This flexibility makes it easy for teams already using these version control systems to adopt Azure Pipelines for their CI/CD needs. Additionally, Azure Pipelines supports parallel builds and testing, which reduces the time required to validate and deploy code, speeding up delivery timelines.

Azure Boards

Azure Boards is a project management tool designed to help teams plan, track, and discuss work across their development lifecycle. It supports Agile methodologies like Scrum and Kanban, providing a flexible environment for teams to visualize their workflows. Azure Boards allows teams to create user stories, track bugs, and manage sprints, giving project managers complete visibility into the development process.

What makes Azure Boards particularly useful is its integration with other Azure DevOps services. For instance, you can link a user story in Azure Boards to a build in Azure Pipelines or a commit in Azure Repos. This helps maintain traceability across the development process, ensuring that each work item is connected to the underlying code and deployment processes. Azure Boards also provides dashboards and reporting features that allow stakeholders to track project progress and team performance in real-time.

Azure Test Plans

Azure Test Plans offers a comprehensive suite of testing tools that enable both manual and automated testing. This service ensures that your application meets quality standards before it is delivered to customers. With Azure Test Plans, you can create test cases, execute tests across various environments, and report on the results. It supports manual testing, exploratory testing, and automated tests using tools like Selenium.

One of the most powerful features of Azure Test Plans is its ability to integrate testing into your CI/CD workflows. You can configure Azure Pipelines to run automated tests at each stage of your pipeline, ensuring that code is thoroughly validated before it is deployed. In addition to automated testing, Azure Test Plans allows for manual tests, which can be particularly useful for user acceptance testing or exploratory testing in complex scenarios.

Azure Artifacts

Azure Artifacts provides a package management service that allows teams to share and consume packages across projects. It supports multiple package types, including NuGet, npm, Maven, and Python. With Azure Artifacts, you can create private or public feeds to manage dependencies for your projects. This is especially useful in large organizations where multiple teams might share common libraries or tools.

Azure Artifacts integrates seamlessly with Azure Pipelines, allowing you to automate the build and release of new packages as part of your CI/CD pipeline. This ensures that teams are always using the latest versions of shared libraries, and it simplifies dependency management across large projects. By incorporating Azure Artifacts into your workflows, you can also enforce version control and track which packages are being used across your applications.

How Azure DevOps Forms a Unified Platform?

Each service provided by Azure DevOps is powerful on its own, but the real strength of the platform comes when they are used together. By integrating Azure Repos, Pipelines, Boards, Test Plans, and Artifacts into a single workflow, you create a unified system where everything from code changes to deployments and testing can be automated and tracked. This level of integration not only simplifies development but also ensures higher quality and faster delivery times.

For example, a developer can push code changes to Azure Repos, which automatically triggers a pipeline in Azure Pipelines. This pipeline can run tests defined in Azure Test Plans and use Azure Artifacts to pull any necessary dependencies. The results of these tests can then be tracked in Azure Boards, giving the entire team visibility into the status of the build. If everything passes, the pipeline can automatically deploy the code to a production environment, completing the process without manual intervention.

Overall, teams can streamline workflows, reduce errors, and focus more on innovation rather than managing infrastructure and processes by using Azure DevOps as a unified platform. Azure DevOps gives teams the power and flexibility they need to build modern software efficiently and scale their operations as they grow.

Setting up Azure DevOps Organization and Projects

The process of setting up an organization (let us consider it as **GitforGits**) and creating a project (such as Spring Boot API) involves a series of steps that will allow you to manage code repositories, CI/CD pipelines, and testing environments efficiently. The process includes to configure your Azure DevOps account, create and manage projects, and establish repositories and pipelines. Additionally, we will also look at how to organize multiple projects within a single organization, which can be helpful for managing larger teams or complex software systems.

Create an Azure DevOps Account

The first step to setting up Azure DevOps is to create an Azure DevOps account if you don't have one already. To do this:

- Navigate to the Azure DevOps homepage (URL: https://azure.microsoft.com/en-us/products/devops/)
- Click on "Start Free" to sign in with your existing Microsoft account or create a new one.
- Once logged in, you will be taken to the Azure DevOps dashboard.

This account will serve as the primary hub for managing your organization and projects. From here, you can define your organization and start setting up your projects and tools.

Setting up Organization

An organization in Azure DevOps acts as a container for multiple projects. For our example, we will create an organization called **GitforGits** as below:

- From the Azure DevOps dashboard, click on "New Organization."
- You will be prompted to create a new organization. Enter **GitforGits** as the name of the organization.
- Select the region where you want your data to be hosted. It's best to choose a region close to your team for better performance.
- Click "Continue."

Your organization **GitforGits** is now created. Organizations help you manage multiple projects under one roof, so if your team works on various applications or modules, you can organize them within this structure.

Setting up a New Project

Once your organization is created, the next step is to set up your Spring Boot API project:

- In the Azure DevOps dashboard, under **GitforGits**, click on "New Project."
- Provide a project name, such as **SpringBootAPI**. You can also add an optional description to describe the purpose of the project.
- Choose the visibility of the project. You can make it public or private, depending on whether you want the project to be accessible to external users.
- Select the version control system. For our project, we will use **Git** as it is widely supported, but Azure DevOps also provides Team Foundation Version Control (TFVC).
- Click "Create."

Once the project is created, Azure DevOps will direct you to the project dashboard, where you can manage the different components such as repositories, pipelines, and boards.

Configuring Repositories

The repository is where your source code will be stored and managed. We will now set up the repository:

- From the project dashboard, click on **Repos** in the left-hand menu.
- Azure DevOps automatically creates an empty Git repository for your project. You can clone this repository or push an existing repository.

- To clone the repository, click on the **Clone** button and copy the URL provided.
- Open a terminal on your local machine, navigate to your desired directory, and run the following command:

```
git clone
https://dev.azure.com/GitforGits/SpringBootAPI/_git/Sprin
gBootAPI
```

- Once cloned, you can add your Spring Boot API code to this repository and push your changes using standard Git commands:

```
git add .

git commit -m "Initial commit"

git push origin master
```

Your source code is now hosted in Azure Repos, ready for building and deploying through Azure Pipelines.

Configuring Pipelines

After setting up your repository, the next step is to configure a CI/CD pipeline that will automate the build and deployment of the application as below:

- In the project dashboard, click on **Pipelines** in the left-hand menu.
- Click "Create Pipeline." Azure DevOps will prompt you to select the source of your code. Choose **Azure Repos Git**.
- Select the **SpringBootAPI** repository and click "Continue."
- Azure DevOps will suggest a default pipeline configuration. Since we're using a Spring Boot project, it will likely suggest a Maven or Gradle pipeline. Select the appropriate build configuration depending on your project's setup.
- Review the YAML configuration file. This file defines the build steps for your project. For a Spring Boot application, the file might look like this:

```
trigger:

- master
```

```
pool:
  vmImage: 'ubuntu-latest'

steps:
- task: Maven@3
  inputs:
    mavenPomFile: 'pom.xml'
    goals: 'clean install'
```

- Save and run the pipeline. Azure Pipelines will automatically pull your source code, build the application, and run any tests you have defined.

Setting up Testing Environments

Testing is an essential part of any DevOps workflow, ensuring that code changes do not introduce bugs or regressions. Azure DevOps integrates with several testing tools and frameworks to automate the testing process. Here is how you can do it:

- In the project dashboard, click on **Test Plans** from the left-hand menu.
- Create a new test plan by clicking "New Test Plan."

You can define manual test cases or integrate automated tests within your pipeline. For example, if you are using JUnit for testing your Spring Boot project, the test cases will automatically run as part of the pipeline.

Now, to configure automated tests, return to **Pipelines** and edit your YAML pipeline file to include test steps:

```
steps:
- script: |
    mvn test
```

```
displayName: 'Run unit tests'
```

Once your pipeline runs, you will see test results integrated within the pipeline run details.

Managing Multiple Projects within an Organization

Azure DevOps makes it easy to manage multiple projects within a single organization. If your team is working on more than one project (such as separate front-end and back-end systems), you can organize them under the same **GitforGits** organization as below:

- From the Azure DevOps dashboard, click on your organization name (**GitforGits**), then select "New Project."
- Create additional projects as needed, following the same steps outlined earlier.

Each project will have its own repositories, pipelines, and boards, but you can manage permissions and access control at the organization level. For example, you can create a shared group of users with access to all projects or limit access to specific teams.

This structure allows you to maintain a clean separation between different applications or modules while ensuring that they all fall under a unified organizational structure.

By adhering to these steps, you have established the GitforGits organization and developed your initial project, SpringBootAPI. You have also gained knowledge in managing repositories, creating testing environments, and setting up CI/CD pipelines. All the subsequent automation, testing, and deployment discussed in the book will build upon this initial setup.

Installing and configuring Azure CLI

Azure Command-Line Interface (CLI) is a powerful tool that allows developers and DevOps professionals to manage Azure resources directly from the command line. Azure CLI provides commands to create, update, and manage resources like virtual machines, storage accounts, Kubernetes clusters, and more. Here we'll show you how to set up Azure CLI on a Windows machine, and then we'll go over some of the most important commands you'll need to run Azure DevOps operations.

Installing Azure CLI on Windows

To begin using Azure CLI, you need to install it on your Windows system as below:

- Visit the official Azure CLI download page.

```
Click on the "Download" button to download the installer
(.msi file) for Windows.
```

- Locate the **.msi** file you just downloaded and run it.
- Follow the on-screen instructions to complete the installation.
- After the installation completes, open a command prompt or PowerShell and type the following command to verify if Azure CLI is installed correctly:

```
az --version
```

This will display the installed version of Azure CLI and confirm that the installation was successful.

Logging into Azure CLI

The next step is to log into your Azure account using Azure CLI. This allows the CLI to authenticate your Azure resources and perform various actions.

- Open the command prompt or PowerShell.
- Enter the following command to log into Azure:

```
az login
```

- A web browser will automatically open, prompting you to enter your Azure credentials. After entering your credentials, the browser will display a confirmation message, and your terminal will show a list of your available subscriptions.

If you have multiple subscriptions, you can select the default subscription by running:

```
az account set --subscription "Your Subscription Name"
```

This ensures that all your Azure CLI commands are executed within the context of the selected subscription.

Configuring Azure CLI

Azure CLI offers several configuration options that make your interaction with Azure more efficient. Some of the most useful configurations include setting default output formats and resource group defaults.

Set Default Output Format

Azure CLI can return output in different formats like json, table, and yaml. To make the output more readable, set it to table format using the following command:

```
az config set defaults.output=table
```

Set Default Resource Group

If you frequently work with the same resource group, it's useful to set a default resource group for your commands. For example:

```
az config set defaults.group=YourResourceGroupName
```

Viewing Current Configurations

You can view your active configurations by running:

```
az config get
```

Popular Azure CLI Commands In-use

Now that Azure CLI is installed and configured, we will cover some of the most commonly used commands for performing DevOps tasks. These commands will help you manage resources, pipelines, and deployments in Azure DevOps.

Creating and Managing Resource Groups

A resource group is a container that holds related Azure resources. The following commands will help you manage resource groups:

- Create a new resource group:

```
az group create --name MyResourceGroup --location eastus
```

- List all resource groups:

```
az group list
```

- Delete a resource group:

```
az group delete --name MyResourceGroup --yes --no-wait
```

Working with Azure Virtual Machines

Virtual machines are a core resource for deploying applications. Following are the steps to create, list, and delete VMs using Azure CLI:

- Create a new virtual machine:

```
az vm create --resource-group MyResourceGroup --name MyVM
--image UbuntuLTS --admin-username azureuser --generate-
ssh-keys
```

- List all VMs:

```
az vm list
```

- Delete a VM:

```
az vm delete --resource-group MyResourceGroup --name MyVM
--yes
```

Managing Azure DevOps Pipelines

Azure CLI also integrates with Azure DevOps to manage CI/CD pipelines and other services. The following commands allow you to interact with your Azure DevOps pipelines:

- Install the Azure DevOps extension:

```
az extension add --name azure-devops
```

- List your pipelines:

```
az pipelines list --organization
https://dev.azure.com/YourOrg --project YourProjectName
```

- Run a pipeline:

```
az pipelines run --name MyPipeline --organization
https://dev.azure.com/YourOrg --project YourProjectName
```

Managing Kubernetes Clusters

If you are working with Kubernetes clusters (AKS), these commands will help you create and manage them.

- Create an AKS cluster:

```
az aks create --resource-group MyResourceGroup --name
MyAKSCluster --node-count 1 --enable-addons monitoring --
generate-ssh-keys
```

- Get Kubernetes credentials for local management:

```
az aks get-credentials --resource-group MyResourceGroup -
-name MyAKSCluster
```

- List AKS clusters:

```
az aks list
```

- Delete an AKS cluster:

```
az aks delete --resource-group MyResourceGroup --name
MyAKSCluster
```

Working with Storage Accounts

Azure Storage accounts are essential for managing blobs, files, and queues. Given below are commands to manage storage:

- Create a storage account:

```
az storage account create --name mystorageaccount --
resource-group MyResourceGroup --location eastus --sku
Standard_LRS
```

- List storage accounts:

```
az storage account list
```

- Delete a storage account:

```
az storage account delete --name mystorageaccount --
resource-group MyResourceGroup
```

Deploying Azure Resources using ARM Templates

Azure CLI makes it easy to deploy infrastructure using ARM templates. These templates define your resources as code, making deployments reproducible.

- Deploy a resource group using an ARM template:

```
az deployment group create --resource-group
MyResourceGroup --template-file azuredeploy.json
```

- List deployments:

```
az deployment group list --resource-group MyResourceGroup
```

- Delete a deployment:

```
az deployment group delete --name MyDeployment --
resource-group MyResourceGroup
```

All these above commands allow you to automate and streamline your DevOps processes directly from the command line. The Azure CLI plays a crucial role in enabling faster, more efficient workflows, and as you progress in the book, you will use it to perform various advanced tasks.

Introduction to Visual Studio Code for DevOps tasks

Visual Studio Code (VS Code) is a powerful and lightweight code editor widely used by developers for various tasks, including DevOps operations. Its versatility, combined with support for extensions and customization, makes it an excellent choice for working in DevOps environments. Now, we will learn to install VS Code on Windows and become familiar with the essential features and components of the editor that will be used throughout your DevOps work.

Installing VS Code on Windows

To start working with VS Code, follow these steps to install it:

- Visit the official Visual Studio Code download page.
- Download the appropriate installer for Windows.
- Open the **.exe** file that you just downloaded and follow the on-screen instructions to install VS Code.
- Ensure that you select the options to add VS Code to your system PATH, which will allow you to open it from the command line using the **code** command.

Once installed, open VS Code by searching for it in the Windows Start Menu or running code in the command line.

VS Code Features and Components for DevOps

VS Code provides numerous features that enhance your DevOps workflows. The following are some essential features and components that you will frequently use in DevOps tasks such as working with source control, CI/CD pipelines, and automation scripts.

Integrated Terminal

The integrated terminal in VS Code allows you to execute commands without leaving the editor, making it highly convenient for running Azure CLI commands, Git commands, or any other command-line tools required for DevOps operations. You can open the terminal by going to **View > Terminal** or by using the shortcut `Ctrl + ``. You can have multiple terminal sessions running simultaneously, each dedicated to different tasks, such as one for Azure CLI and another for Git commands.

This feature is particularly useful when you are working on automation scripts, interacting with Docker, or deploying infrastructure using Infrastructure as Code (IaC) tools like Terraform.

Git Integration

VS Code comes with built-in Git support, making it easy to manage source control without needing to switch to another Git client. This feature is vital when working with code repositories in Azure Repos or GitHub.

- Cloning Repositories

You can clone a repository directly from VS Code. Simply click on Source Control in the left sidebar, then click on Clone Repository. Enter the URL of the repository you want to clone (such as the one from Azure Repos).

- Commit, Push, and Pull

The Source Control pane also provides easy access to common Git actions like committing, pushing, and pulling changes. This is where you can stage files, write commit messages, and sync changes with the remote repository.

- Branch Management

You can create and switch between branches, making it convenient to work on different features or bug fixes in isolated environments before merging the code.

Extensions for Azure and DevOps

VS Code's extensibility is one of its biggest strengths, and you can enhance your workflow by adding several extensions specifically designed for Azure DevOps tasks. Following are some key extensions that you will use:

- Azure Account

This extension allows you to sign in to your Azure account from within VS Code. Once signed in, you can access all your Azure subscriptions and resources without needing to switch to the Azure portal.

Install it by going to the Extensions Marketplace (on the left sidebar) and searching for Azure Account. Once installed, you can sign in by running the Azure: Sign In command from the Command Palette (Ctrl + Shift + P).

- Azure CLI Tools

This extension enhances the usage of Azure CLI by providing syntax highlighting, IntelliSense, and autocompletion for Azure CLI commands. It is useful when writing scripts or commands to interact with Azure resources such as virtual machines, storage accounts, or Kubernetes clusters.

- Azure Pipelines

The **Azure Pipelines** extension allows you to manage your CI/CD pipelines directly from VS Code. You can create, edit, and run pipelines for your projects without switching to the Azure DevOps portal.

This extension is particularly useful when working with YAML-based pipelines, as it provides support for IntelliSense and schema validation for the pipeline files.

- Docker

Many DevOps workflows involve containerization. The Docker extension in VS Code provides a convenient way to work with Docker containers and images. You can view running containers, build images, and run Docker commands without leaving the editor. You can install the Docker extension to manage containers and images right from the left-hand sidebar.

Editing and Managing YAML Pipelines

Azure DevOps allows you to define CI/CD pipelines as code using YAML, and VS Code provides an excellent environment for editing these YAML files.

- YAML Support

VS Code has built-in support for YAML files, and the **Azure Pipelines** extension adds enhanced capabilities, including schema validation and IntelliSense for the available pipeline commands.

This feature is invaluable when creating multi-stage pipelines, as it helps ensure that your syntax is correct and that all steps in the pipeline are properly defined.

- Linting and Formatting

When working with YAML files, ensuring consistent formatting is essential. VS Code provides automatic linting and formatting tools to help you maintain clean and readable pipeline files.

Task Automation with Task Runner

VS Code's task runner allows you to automate repetitive tasks like building projects, running tests, or executing scripts. In a DevOps environment, this feature can be particularly useful for running deployment scripts or testing configurations.

- Defining Tasks

You can define tasks in a **.vscode/tasks.json** file, specifying commands you frequently run. For example, you can set up a task to deploy your Spring Boot API to Azure by calling Azure CLI commands.

- Running Tasks

Tasks can be executed by going to Terminal > Run Task, or you can assign keybindings to your most frequently used tasks.

Remote Development

In many DevOps scenarios, you might be required to work with remote environments or containers. The **Remote - SSH** and **Remote - Containers** extensions make it easy to connect to and develop within remote environments or Docker containers.

- Remote - SSH

This extension allows you to connect to remote servers using SSH directly from VS Code. You can run your development tasks on cloud-based virtual machines as if they were local.

- Remote - Containers

The **Remote - Containers** extension enables you to develop within a Docker container, which is especially useful for teams working with containerized applications. You can connect to a running container, edit files, and run tests without having to manually enter the container's environment.

As you continue through this book, you will see how these components are used in conjunction with Azure CLI, Azure Pipelines, and other tools to implement a seamless DevOps environment.

Cloning and Setting up REST API Application

As we go through the different DevOps processes, like continuous integration, deployment, and testing, you'll be able to work on a real-world project by cloning this application. Now, we will walk you through cloning the project repository to your local environment, configuring it in VS Code, and preparing it for future use with Azure DevOps.

Cloning the Spring Boot REST API Repository

Cloning a repository means creating a local copy of the source code that is stored remotely. In this case, we will use Git to clone the Spring Boot REST API example repository from GitHub to your local machine. The repository for the Spring Boot REST API can be found at the following URL: https://github.com/bezkoder/spring-boot-3-rest-api-example

- Open the terminal in VS Code by going to View > Terminal or using the shortcut `Ctrl + ``.
- In the terminal, navigate to the directory where you want to clone the repository by running the following command:

```
cd path/to/your/folder
```

- Use the **git clone** command to clone the repository:

```
git clone https://github.com/bezkoder/spring-boot-3-rest-
api-example.git
```

This will create a local copy of the repository on your machine, and you will see the project files in the Explorer pane of VS Code.

Opening Project in VS Code

Now that you have cloned the repository, the next step is to open and configure the project in VS Code:

- In VS Code, click on **File > Open Folder** and navigate to the directory where the repository was cloned.
- Select the folder and click "Open." This will load the Spring Boot API project into VS Code, and you should see all the project files displayed in the Explorer pane. The key files and directories you will be working with are:
    - **src/main/java**: This folder contains the Java source code for the API.
    - **pom.xml**: This is the Maven build file, which includes project dependencies, build configurations, and plugins.
    - **application.properties**: Located in **src/main/resources**, this file contains configuration settings for the Spring Boot application.

Since this is a Java-based project, you need to ensure you have the necessary Java development extensions installed in VS Code. You can do this by searching for and installing the Java Extension Pack from the Extensions Marketplace. This extension pack includes important tools such as the Java Language Server and Maven support, which will be crucial as you start working on the Spring Boot API.

Building the Application

Before running the application, you need to ensure that it builds correctly. This step will also allow you to verify that all dependencies are installed. You can use the following command to build the project using Maven:

```
mvn clean install
```

Maven will download any necessary dependencies and compile the project. If the build is successful, you will see a BUILD SUCCESS message in the terminal.

If the build fails, check the error messages to ensure all dependencies are correctly defined in the pom.xml file. Common issues include missing dependencies or incorrect versions.

Running the Application Locally

Once the project has been successfully built, you can run the Spring Boot application locally to ensure it is working as expected. For this, use the following command to run the Spring Boot application:

```
mvn spring-boot:run
```

This will start the embedded Tomcat server, and you should see output in the terminal indicating that the server is running on **http://localhost:8080**.

Accessing the API:

Open a web browser and navigate to http://localhost:8080. If the application is running successfully, you should be able to interact with the REST API endpoints.

You can use curl to test the API endpoints. For example, to test a GET request, you can use:

```
curl http://localhost:8080/api/example
```

Preparing Project for Azure DevOps

The Spring Boot REST API application is now cloned, built, and running locally. The next step is to prepare it for integration with Azure DevOps, where it will be part of a CI/CD pipeline.

To start using Azure DevOps, you will need to push the cloned repository to Azure Repos (or any other Git repository service you are using in Azure DevOps).

Open the integrated terminal and add the remote repository from Azure DevOps:

```
git remote add azure
https://dev.azure.com/YourOrgName/YourProjectName/_git/Yo
urRepoName
```

Push the local code to Azure Repos:

```
git push -u azure master
```

Once the code is in Azure Repos, you can set up a YAML pipeline (we will learn about YAML in detail in the next chapter) to automate the build and deployment processes. This involves creating a azure-pipelines.yml file in the root directory of your project that defines the build and deployment stages.

Following is a quick basic YAML configuration you can use for Azure Pipelines:

```
trigger:

- master
```

```
pool:
  vmImage: 'ubuntu-latest'

steps:
- task: Maven@3
  inputs:
    mavenPomFile: 'pom.xml'
    goals: 'clean install'
- task: Maven@3
  inputs:    mavenPomFile: 'pom.xml'
    goals: 'spring-boot:run'
```

This YAML file configures a build process where the code is compiled and tested, followed by running the application as part of the pipeline.

With this, you learned how to build and run the application locally, and we prepared it for integration with Azure DevOps by pushing the code to Azure Repos. This setup will be used in upcoming chapters where we automate build and deployment processes using Azure Pipelines.

Summary

Overall, we focused on understanding and configuring Azure DevOps by learning about Azure DevOps, including how it integrates services such as Azure Repos, Pipelines, Boards, Test Plans, and Artifacts into a unified platform for managing DevOps operations. We then set up an organization called GitforGits in Azure DevOps and started a project to manage the Spring Boot API application. This included configuring the Azure DevOps account, creating Git repositories, and preparing the environment for future builds and deployments.

We also installed and configured Azure CLI on a Windows machine, allowing us to interact with Azure services via the command line. Several common DevOps commands, such as managing resource groups, virtual machines, and Kubernetes clusters, were introduced. Finally, we cloned the Spring Boot REST API sample application from GitHub and imported it into VS Code. This process included configuring the necessary development tools and preparing the application for integration with Azure Pipelines, which automates builds and deployments. The chapter provided a solid groundwork for utilizing Azure DevOps to put DevOps workflows into practice.

Chapter 2: Pipeline as Code with YAML

Overview

Pipeline as Code allows you to define your entire CI/CD workflow as a code file, which simplifies version control, sharing, and automation. In this chapter, we will explore the concept of Pipeline as Code and how it is implemented in Azure Pipelines using YAML. YAML is a popular format for defining pipeline steps, environments, and dependencies because it is both simple and powerful. You will learn the syntax and structure of YAML to define pipelines. We will look at how YAML works in Azure Pipelines and how it can help manage the build, testing, and release stages of the development cycle, with a focus on the Spring Boot API application.

This chapter also covers how to create a Spring Boot build pipeline using YAML. You will learn how to set up a basic build pipeline, automate code compilation, run unit tests, and package your application for deployment. We will also talk about multi-stage pipelines, which are necessary for managing more complex workflows with multiple environments (such as development, staging, and production) in a single pipeline. Lastly, you will learn how to use VS Code to edit and manage YAML files. This includes installing necessary extensions to make writing and validating YAML syntax easier, ensuring a smooth experience when creating and maintaining pipelines. After this chapter, you will understand Pipeline as Code and how to use YAML to automate continuous integration and delivery.

Introduction to Pipeline as Code

Traditionally, managing pipelines was done through graphical user interfaces (GUIs), where configurations would be manually set. However, with Pipeline as Code, these configurations are written in code, stored in version control systems like Git, and treated as part of the overall project source code. This shift brings automation, repeatability, and greater control over the build and release process, which are essential in modern DevOps practices.

With Pipeline as Code, the entire CI/CD process becomes highly manageable, as every stage of the pipeline—from building, testing, and deploying software—can be described in a file. This file is then stored and version-controlled just like any other piece of code in a project. The benefits are clear: teams can collaborate on pipeline definitions, review changes, track the history of updates, and even rollback to previous pipeline versions if necessary. Moreover, Pipeline as Code allows for the automation of complex workflows that might involve multiple teams, environments, and technologies, all in a streamlined manner.

One of the core concepts in Pipeline as Code is the **declarative nature** of pipelines. Declarative pipelines specify **what** steps should be executed without focusing on **how** they are performed. For example, rather than scripting each individual step in a pipeline, a declarative approach lets you define the overall structure, such as building, testing, and deployment, while the pipeline engine handles the details of execution. This reduces the complexity of managing pipelines and enables faster changes and iteration.

Another important concept is **version control integration**. Because pipelines are written as code, they can be versioned alongside the application source code. This means that changes to pipelines can be tracked, reviewed, and approved through the same mechanisms used for application development. Teams can ensure that pipeline updates are tested and validated before being merged into the production pipeline, thereby reducing the risks of deployment failures caused by incorrect pipeline configurations.

Pipeline as Code also enables **IaC** practices, where the underlying infrastructure (e.g., servers, databases, and networks) is also defined and managed through code. In combination with tools like Terraform or Azure Resource Manager templates, you can automate the provisioning of environments alongside application deployments, providing a fully automated pipeline from code changes to running infrastructure in production.

Introduction to YAML in Pipeline as Code

YAML (short for "YAML Ain't Markup Language") is the language typically used to define pipeline configurations in Azure DevOps and many other CI/CD platforms. YAML is a human-readable data serialization format that is both easy to write and parse, making it a popular choice for defining configuration files in DevOps workflows. In the context of Pipeline as Code, YAML is used to describe the various stages, jobs, and tasks that need to be executed in the pipeline.

The simplicity of YAML lies in its structure. It uses indentation to represent hierarchy, allowing you to easily define the relationships between different elements of a pipeline. For example, you can group related tasks together under the same stage or job and control the flow of execution in a clear, logical manner. YAML's focus on readability and minimal syntax makes it accessible to teams with varying levels of experience, allowing developers, DevOps engineers, and operations teams to collaborate on pipeline definitions.

One of the key benefits of using YAML for Pipeline as Code is **modularity**. In YAML, you can reuse blocks of code by defining templates or parameters, which help reduce redundancy in pipeline configurations. For instance, if you have multiple stages in your pipeline that follow similar patterns, such as building and testing across different environments, you can define these steps once and reuse them across the pipeline. This not only makes the pipeline easier to manage but also reduces the likelihood of errors when updating or extending the pipeline.

YAML also supports **conditional logic**, which allows you to control which stages or jobs in the pipeline should be executed based on certain conditions. For example, you might want to run tests only when changes are made to specific parts of the codebase, or you might want to deploy to production only when certain approval gates have been passed. With YAML, you can easily define these rules, ensuring that your pipeline runs efficiently and meets the needs of different environments.

In addition to its flexibility, YAML's **integration with version control** systems like Git makes it ideal for managing pipelines in DevOps environments. Because pipeline configurations are stored as YAML files in the source code repository, they can be versioned, branched, and reviewed just like any other piece of code. This ensures that changes to the pipeline are fully transparent and traceable, enabling teams to iterate quickly while maintaining control over their CI/CD processes.

For example, in Azure DevOps, the YAML file (already shown in the previous chapter) used to define a pipeline might look like this:

```
trigger:

  - master


pool:

  vmImage: 'ubuntu-latest'


steps:

  - task: Maven@3

    inputs:

      mavenPomFile: 'pom.xml'

      goals: 'clean install'


  - task: PublishBuildArtifacts@1

    inputs:

      PathtoPublish: '$(Build.ArtifactStagingDirectory)'

      ArtifactName: 'drop'
```

In this simple YAML example, we are defining a pipeline that triggers when there is a change to the **master** branch. The pipeline uses an Ubuntu virtual machine to run the tasks, which include building the application using Maven and publishing the build artifacts. Each task is clearly defined with inputs and outputs, making it easy to understand the flow of the pipeline.

Additionally, YAML's **platform agnosticism** makes it a versatile tool for defining pipelines across different CI/CD platforms. While Azure DevOps, GitLab, Jenkins, and others each have their own specific syntax and configurations, YAML's core principles remain the same. This means that once you are familiar with writing pipelines in YAML, you can easily adapt to different CI/CD systems without needing to learn entirely new tools or interfaces.

Finally, YAML's **compatibility with cloud services** like Azure, AWS, and Google Cloud enables seamless integration with infrastructure provisioning and management tasks. For example, you can use YAML to define pipelines that automatically deploy code to virtual machines, Kubernetes clusters, or serverless environments in the cloud. This tight integration between YAML pipelines and cloud infrastructure allows teams to build fully automated, scalable workflows that cover the entire software delivery lifecycle.

Benefits of YAML in Pipeline as Code

One of the main advantages of using YAML for Pipeline as Code is its **human-readability**. Because YAML is designed to be easy for humans to read and write, it reduces the cognitive overhead associated with managing complex CI/CD pipelines. Developers and DevOps engineers can quickly understand the pipeline configuration, troubleshoot issues, and make changes without needing to consult extensive documentation or rely on proprietary tools.

YAML also promotes **collaboration**. By treating pipeline definitions as code and storing them in version control, teams can collaborate on pipeline changes just as they would on application code. This enables peer reviews, automated testing, and rollbacks for pipeline configurations, ensuring that changes are thoroughly vetted before being applied in production environments.

Another important benefit is **automation**. YAML pipelines are fully automated, allowing for hands-off execution of CI/CD processes once the pipeline is defined. Teams can define triggers, such as code pushes or pull requests, and let the pipeline automatically handle the building, testing, and deployment of applications. This reduces the need for manual intervention, increases efficiency, and minimizes the risk of human error.

Finally, YAML's **declarative nature** aligns well with modern DevOps practices. Rather than scripting each individual step, teams can focus on defining the desired outcomes of their pipelines, letting the underlying system handle the execution details. This makes pipelines easier to maintain, especially as applications and infrastructure evolve over time.

By the end of this chapter, you will have a deep understanding of how YAML enables Pipeline as Code, providing a flexible, powerful, and efficient way to automate CI/CD workflows. You will also see how the declarative nature of YAML simplifies the management of complex pipelines, helping to ensure that builds, tests, and deployments are consistent, repeatable, and scalable.

Exploring YAML for Azure Pipelines

Here, in this section, we will explore how to use **YAML** to define an Azure pipeline for our **Spring Boot REST API** project.

Creating Pipeline Definition File

The first step is to create a YAML file that will define the pipeline. In Azure DevOps, the standard practice is to name the file **azure-pipelines.yml** and store it in the root directory of your project repository. This file will contain all the steps your pipeline needs to execute.

To create the azure-pipelines.yml file:

- In VS Code, open your Spring Boot project folder.
- In the root directory of your project, create a new file called azure-pipelines.yml.

This YAML file will hold all the instructions that Azure Pipelines will follow to automate the build and deployment processes.

Defining Triggers

Triggers in Azure Pipelines specify when the pipeline should run. For example, you might want the pipeline to run automatically every time a commit is made to the **master** branch.

To define a trigger in YAML:

```
trigger:

  - master
```

This simple trigger configuration means that the pipeline will run every time there is a push to the **master** branch. You can also specify other branches if you want to trigger builds on multiple branches.

Specifying Pipeline Environment

Azure Pipelines uses virtual machines (VMs) to run your jobs. These VMs can be Windows, Linuor macOS. Since we are working with a Java-based Spring Boot project, we will use an Ubuntu machine for our pipeline:

```
pool:

  vmImage: 'ubuntu-latest'
```

This tells Azure Pipelines to use the latest Ubuntu VM image for running the pipeline. If needed, you can switch to a different image (e.g., **windows-latest** for Windows-based pipelines).

Defining the Build Stage

The build stage is where the code is compiled, and any necessary tests are run. Since we are using Maven to build the Spring Boot project, the **steps** section will define the tasks needed to build the project.

Following is how you can define the build stage using Maven in the **azure-pipelines.yml** file:

```
steps:

- task: Maven@3

  inputs:

    mavenPomFile: 'pom.xml'

    goals: 'clean install'
```

In the above script,

- **task** refers to the task that Azure Pipelines will execute. In this case, **Maven@3** tells Azure Pipelines to use the Maven task.
- **mavenPomFile** specifies the location of the **pom.xml** file, which is used by Maven to manage dependencies and build the project.
- **goals** are the Maven goals to be executed. In this, we are using clean install, which first cleans any existing build artifacts and then compiles and packages the code.

Running Unit Tests

With Maven, we can automatically run unit tests during the build process. If your Spring Boot project contains unit tests, they will be automatically executed when you run the Maven **install** goal. Now, to ensure that the test results are recorded in Azure Pipelines, you can add the following step to publish the test results:

```
- task: PublishTestResults@2

  inputs:

    testResultsFormat: 'JUnit'
```

```
    testResultsFiles: '**/surefire-reports/TEST-*.xml'
    failTaskOnFailedTests: true
```

In this above script,

- **PublishTestResults@2** is the task for publishing test results in Azure Pipelines.
- **testResultsFormat** specifies the format of the test results.
- **testResultsFiles** tells the pipeline where to find the test result files, typically in the **surefire-reports** folder generated by Maven.
- **failTaskOnFailedTests** ensures that the pipeline fails if any tests do not pass, alerting the team to fix the issues before proceeding to deployment.

Defining Build Artifacts

Once the application is built and tested, you need to package and publish the build artifacts (e.g., the .jar file) so they can be used in later stages of the pipeline, such as deployment.

To do this, add the following task to publish the build artifacts:

```
- task: PublishBuildArtifacts@1
  inputs:
    PathtoPublish: '$(Build.ArtifactStagingDirectory)'
    ArtifactName: 'drop'
    publishLocation: 'Container'
```

In the above task code,

- **PathtoPublish** specifies the location of the build artifacts that should be published. In this case, we use **$(Build.ArtifactStagingDirectory),** which is a predefined variable in Azure Pipelines.
- **ArtifactName** defines the name of the artifact that will be created.
- **publishLocation** sets where the artifacts will be stored (in this case, in a container within Azure DevOps).

Running the Pipeline in Azure DevOps

Once you've defined your **azure-pipelines.yml** file, it's time to run the pipeline in Azure DevOps.

Now, to push the YAML file to Azure Repos:

- Open the terminal in VS Code and run the following commands to push the YAML file to Azure Repos:

```
git add azure-pipelines.yml

git commit -m "Add pipeline configuration"

git push origin master
```

For creating the Pipeline in Azure DevOps:

- In Azure DevOps, navigate to **Pipelines** in your project.
- Click **New Pipeline** and select **Azure Repos Git** as the source.
- Select your repository and branch (e.g., **master**).

Azure DevOps will automatically detect the **azure-pipelines.yml** file and use it to create the pipeline.

To run the Pipeline:

- Once the pipeline is created, click **Run** to trigger the pipeline.
- You can monitor the pipeline's progress through the Azure DevOps interface, where you will see each step executed in real-time.

After the pipeline finishes running, Azure DevOps provides detailed logs for each step in the pipeline, including build status, test results, and artifact publishing.

Modifying the Pipeline

One of the benefits of Pipeline as Code is the ability to modify the pipeline easily through the **azure-pipelines.yml** file. If you need to add new stages, modify existing tasks, or change the build environment, simply edit the YAML file in your repository.

For example, if you want to add a **staging environment** for deploying your application, you could define a new stage in the YAML file like this:

```
stages:
```

```
- stage: Build
  jobs:
  - job: BuildApp
    steps:
    - task: Maven@3
      inputs:
        mavenPomFile: 'pom.xml'
        goals: 'clean install'

- stage: DeployToStaging
  jobs:
  - deployment: DeployStaging
    environment: 'staging'
    strategy:
      runOnce:
        deploy:
          steps:
          - script: echo "Deploying to staging
environment"
```

This defines two stages: **Build** and **DeployToStaging**. The second stage will only execute after the build stage is successfully completed.

Overall, you learned how to create and configure the **azure-pipelines.yml** file, define build and test steps, publish artifacts, and run the pipeline in Azure DevOps. And we can surely conclude that YAML allows for a flexible and modular pipeline definition, which can be easily modified as your project evolves.

Creating Build Pipeline for Spring Boot

Creating a build pipeline for a **Spring Boot** application in Azure DevOps involves defining a series of automated steps to compile, test, and package the application. Since we already discussed the basic YAML structure in the previous section, we will now practically create the build pipeline for the **Spring Boot REST API** project from scratch. This pipeline will compile the Java code, run unit tests, and publish the build artifacts.

Create a New Pipeline in Azure DevOps

- Navigate to Pipelines:
    - From the left-hand menu, click on **Pipelines**.
    - Click on **New Pipeline** to begin the process of creating a new build pipeline.
- Select the Source for the Pipeline:
    - Azure DevOps will ask where your code is hosted. Since we are using Azure Repos Git, select **Azure Repos Git**.
    - Choose your repository (e.g., **SpringBootAPI**).
    - Once selected, Azure DevOps will automatically detect your repository and proceed to the next step.
- Configure the Pipeline:
    - Choose **YAML** as the pipeline configuration format. Azure DevOps will try to suggest some default templates, but we will create our pipeline manually in this case.
    - Select **Starter Pipeline** to begin with a blank pipeline.

Writing the Build Pipeline for Spring Boot

With the YAML starter pipeline in place, you can now start defining the actual build steps required to compile, test, and package the Spring Boot application. The following configuration defines a basic build pipeline using Maven:

```
trigger:

- master
```

```yaml
pool:

  vmImage: 'ubuntu-latest'

steps:

- task: Maven@3

  inputs:

    mavenPomFile: 'pom.xml'

    goals: 'clean install'
```

In the above script, **mavenPomFile** points to the **pom.xml** file, which contains the dependencies and build configuration for the Spring Boot application.

Once the application is built, you will need to package and publish the **.jar** or **.war** file as a build artifact for later deployment stages.

```yaml
- task: PublishBuildArtifacts@1

  inputs:

    PathtoPublish: '$(Build.ArtifactStagingDirectory)'

    ArtifactName: 'drop'

    publishLocation: 'Container'
```

Here,

- **PathtoPublish** points to the directory where the build artifacts (the compiled .jar file) are located.
- **ArtifactName** is the name of the published artifact (in this case, **drop**).
- **publishLocation** specifies that the artifacts will be stored in Azure DevOps's artifact container for future use in other stages like deployment.

Configuring Unit Testing

After this, Azure DevOps will run tests during the build process automatically. However, you can explicitly tell Azure Pipelines to publish the test results so that they are displayed in the pipeline run summary:

```
- task: PublishTestResults@2
  inputs:
    testResultsFormat: 'JUnit'
    testResultsFiles: '**/surefire-reports/TEST-*.xml'
    failTaskOnFailedTests: true
```

In the above script,

- **PublishTestResults@2** tells Azure DevOps to publish the results of any tests that are run.
- **testResultsFormat** specifies that the test results are in JUnit format, which is standard for Maven projects.
- **testResultsFiles** specifies the location of the test result files, usually located in the **surefire-reports** folder when using Maven.
- **failTaskOnFailedTests** ensures that the pipeline fails if any unit tests do not pass, which is essential for maintaining code quality.

Saving and Running the Pipeline

Once the YAML configuration is complete, you need to save and run the pipeline. To save the YAML file:

- In Azure DevOps, click **Save**.
- Commit the **azure-pipelines.yml** file to your repository. This file will now be part of the repository, and any changes made to it in the future can be tracked via Git.

After saving the pipeline, Azure DevOps will automatically trigger the first run. You can then monitor the progress of the pipeline through the Azure DevOps interface. Each step (trigger, build, test, and publish) will be displayed in real time. Once the pipeline run is complete, Azure DevOps will display the results of the build and tests.

You can view detailed logs for each task, check if the unit tests passed, and download the build artifacts (the compiled Spring Boot .jar file).

Modifying the Pipeline

As your project grows, you may need to modify the build pipeline to accommodate new requirements or environments. For example, if you introduce new testing frameworks or need to deploy the application to different environments, you can simply update the **azure-pipelines.yml** file.

Also, to add additional build stages, or to deploy the application to a staging or production environment, you would modify the YAML file to include more stages and steps.

For instance, you could add deployment steps like this:

```
- stage: DeployToStaging

  jobs:

   - job: Deploy

     steps:

     - script: echo "Deploying to Staging Environment"
```

This stage can be configured to deploy the Spring Boot application to Azure App Service, virtual machines, or Kubernetes clusters as needed.

With this, you have now successfully created a build pipeline from scratch for the Spring Boot REST API project. The pipeline compiles the project, runs unit tests, and publishes the build artifacts, all within a fully automated process in Azure DevOps. As you progress through the book, you will learn to expand this pipeline to include more advanced stages, such as automated deployments and integration tests to have complete control over the application's lifecycle from code to production.

Structuring Multi-Stage YAML Pipelines

Multi-stage pipelines are essential when you have a complex workflow that involves different stages like **development**, **staging**, and **production**. Each of these stages can be configured to handle different tasks, such as building, testing, and deploying the application to separate environments. In this section, we will explore how to structure a **multi-stage YAML pipeline** in Azure DevOps.

Define Structure of Multi-Stage Pipelines

In a multi-stage pipeline, you define the pipeline stages explicitly. Each stage can contain jobs, and jobs can contain tasks. Stages are executed sequentially, and each stage can have specific conditions, environments, and approvals.

The basic structure of a multi-stage pipeline looks like this:

```
stages:
- stage: Build
  jobs:
  - job: BuildJob
    steps:
    - script: echo "Building the application"

- stage: Staging
  jobs:
  - job: DeployToStaging
    steps:
    - script: echo "Deploying to Staging Environment"

- stage: Production
  jobs:
  - job: DeployToProduction
    steps:
    - script: echo "Deploying to Production Environment"
```

This pipeline has three stages: **Build**, **Staging**, and **Production**. Each stage contains one job, and within each job, there are steps that define the tasks to be executed. We will now expand this basic structure to handle a real-world example for our Spring Boot application.

Defining Build Stage

The **Build** stage is responsible for compiling the Spring Boot application, running unit tests, and publishing the build artifacts. We will reuse some of the YAML we introduced in the previous sections to define the Build stage.

```
stages:

- stage: Build

  displayName: "Build the Spring Boot Application"

  jobs:

  - job: BuildJob

    displayName: "Build and Test"

    pool:

      vmImage: 'ubuntu-latest'

    steps:

    - task: Maven@3

      inputs:

        mavenPomFile: 'pom.xml'

        goals: 'clean install'

    - task: PublishBuildArtifacts@1

      inputs:

        PathtoPublish:
'$(Build.ArtifactStagingDirectory)'
```

```
        ArtifactName: 'drop'
```

Following is what happens in this **Build** stage:

- **pool** specifies the virtual machine image to use (Ubuntu in this case).
- **Maven@3** is used to compile and test the Spring Boot project, running the **clean install** goal.
- **PublishBuildArtifacts@1** packages the .jar file and makes it available for future stages, such as deployment.

Defining Staging

Once the application is built, the next logical step is to deploy it to a **staging environment**. The staging environment is typically used for testing and quality assurance before deploying to production. In this stage, we will define a job to deploy the application to a temporary environment, such as **Azure App Service** or **AKS**.

```
- stage: Staging
  displayName: "Deploy to Staging"
  dependsOn: Build
  condition: succeeded()
  jobs:
  - deployment: DeployToStaging
    displayName: "Deploy to Staging Environment"
    environment: 'staging'
    strategy:
      runOnce:
        deploy:
          steps:
```

```
      - download: current

      - script: echo "Deploying Spring Boot
application to Staging"

      - task: AzureWebApp@1

        inputs:

          azureSubscription: 'Your Azure
Subscription'

          appName: 'spring-boot-staging'

          package: $(Pipeline.Workspace)/drop/*.jar
```

In this stage,

- **dependsOn: Build** ensures that the Staging stage will only run if the Build stage succeeds.
- **condition: succeeded()** further ensures that the stage runs only if the previous stage completes without errors.
- **environment: 'staging'** specifies that this job is associated with the staging environment.
- **download: current** downloads the build artifacts (i.e., the **.jar** file) from the Build stage.

AzureWebApp@1 is an Azure task that deploys the application to Azure App Service. You can substitute this with other deployment tasks if you are using a different service (like Azure Kubernetes Service or a virtual machine).

Defining Production Stage

The **Production** stage is where the application is deployed to the live production environment. This stage often includes additional safeguards like approval gates or manual checks to ensure everything is in place before deployment. We will add the deployment task and configure the environment similarly to the Staging stage.

```
- stage: Production

  displayName: "Deploy to Production"

  dependsOn: Staging
```

```
  condition: succeeded()

  jobs:

  - deployment: DeployToProduction

    displayName: "Deploy to Production Environment"

    environment: 'production'

    strategy:

      runOnce:

        deploy:

          steps:

            - download: current

            - script: echo "Deploying Spring Boot
application to Production"

            - task: AzureWebApp@1

              inputs:

                azureSubscription: 'Your Azure
Subscription'

                appName: 'spring-boot-production'

                package: $(Pipeline.Workspace)/drop/*.jar
```

In this stage, it depends on the successful completion of the **Staging** stage (**dependsOn: Staging**). The **AzureWebApp@1** task deploys the application to the production instance of Azure App Service, just like it did for staging, but with the production environment details.

Running and Monitoring the Multi-stage Pipeline

After defining the multi-stage pipeline in the **azure-pipelines.yml** file, push the file to the Azure

Repos Git repository:

```
git add azure-pipelines.yml

git commit -m "Add multi-stage pipeline"

git push origin master
```

Once the pipeline is in place,

- Azure DevOps will automatically trigger the pipeline based on your defined triggers (e.g., when pushing to the **master** branch).
- You can monitor the pipeline in the Azure DevOps **Pipelines** section, where each stage—Build, Staging, and Production—will be displayed with real-time logs.
- Review the build logs, test results, and deployment status for each stage.

This structured multi-stage YAML pipeline ensures that the application is built, tested, and deployed sequentially across **development**, **staging**, and **production** environments, all within a single pipeline. Each stage is clearly defined, and the pipeline executes each step in a controlled and automated manner.

Using VS Code extensions for YAML

If you want to be more productive and make sure your YAML files are syntactically correct, use VS Code with extensions made for YAML. Here we'll take a look at a few of the best VS Code extensions that make working with YAML files easier, including adding validation and editing features.

We will set up a multi-stage YAML pipeline earlier, and these tools will help you work on it.

Installing the YAML Extension in VS Code

The most important extension for working with YAML files in VS Code is the **YAML extension**. It provides syntax highlighting, autocompletion, and validation support, helping you avoid errors in your pipeline configuration.

To install the YAML Extension:

- Open VS Code.
- Go to the **Extensions Marketplace** by clicking the square icon on the left sidebar or pressing **Ctrl + Shift + X**.

- In the search bar, type **YAML** and select the extension developed by **Red Hat**.
- Click **Install** to add the extension to your workspace. This extension will enable basic YAML functionalities such as:
    - **Syntax Highlighting**: Automatically highlights YAML syntax for better readability.
    - **Autocompletion**: Offers suggestions for YAML keywords and structure as you type.
    - **Error Highlighting**: Points out syntax errors in real-time, making it easier to identify and fix issues as you write YAML files.

Installing Azure Pipelines Extension

To work specifically with **Azure Pipelines**, you should install the **Azure Pipelines extension** in VS Code. This extension enhances YAML file editing for Azure Pipelines by providing schema validation and integration with Azure DevOps.

To install Azure Pipelines Extension:

- Open the Extensions Marketplace (**Ctrl + Shift + X**).
- Search for Azure Pipelines.
- Install the extension by **Microsoft**. With this extension, you will get:
    - **Schema validation**: Ensures that your pipeline YAML files conform to the correct structure and syntax for Azure Pipelines.
    - **IntelliSense support**: Provides autocompletion and suggestions for Azure-specific tasks and settings when writing your pipeline files.
    - **Pipeline status updates**: You can check the status of pipelines directly from within VS Code and view logs and details of pipeline executions.

Leveraging IntelliSense for YAML files

One of the biggest advantages of using VS Code with the **YAML** and **Azure Pipelines** extensions is the **IntelliSense** feature, which offers smart suggestions as you type. IntelliSense improves both speed and accuracy when working with complex pipeline configurations.

For example, when you are typing a task in your **azure-pipelines.yml** file, IntelliSense can suggest the next valid option, reducing the chances of making errors. As you start typing **- task:**, IntelliSense will automatically provide a dropdown list of available tasks like **Maven@3**, **PublishBuildArtifacts@1**, or **AzureWebApp@1**.

And, once you select a task, it will also suggest the available parameters for that task, such as inputs for configuring Maven goals or paths for publishing artifacts.

Enabling YAML Linting and Formatting

The **YAML extension** supports linting and formatting, making it easier to keep your files clean and readable. The YAML extension provides real-time linting for your YAML files. It will automatically highlight issues such as improper indentation, missing colons, or invalid syntax.

You can also configure custom linting rules by modifying your VS Code settings. Open the Command Palette (**Ctrl + Shift + P**), type **Preferences: Open Settings (JSON)**, and add YAML-specific configurations like:

```
"yaml.customTags": [

  "!Base64 scalar",

  "!Ref sequence"

]
```

You can automatically format your YAML files by installing the **Prettier - Code Formatter** extension:

- Search for **Prettier** in the Extensions Marketplace.
- Install it and configure it as your default formatter for YAML files.
- To format your YAML files, right-click on the file and select **Format Document** or press **Shift + Alt + F**.

This will enforce consistent indentation and structure across all your YAML files.

Using Snippets for faster YAML Editing

Snippet Overview

Snippets are predefined code templates that can be invoked with a few keystrokes, saving time and reducing repetitive typing. **YAML Snippets** can help you quickly insert commonly used blocks of code into your YAML files. You can either use existing snippets or create custom ones.

To install the YAML Snippets Extension, search for **YAML Snippets** in the Extensions Marketplace and install it. This extension provides quick templates for common YAML structures like stages, jobs, tasks, and more.

Creating Custom Snippets

If there are specific sections of your YAML pipeline that you frequently reuse, such as deployment steps or task configurations, you can define custom snippets in VS Code.

To create custom snippets, go to **File > Preferences > User Snippets**, then select **YAML**.

Following is an example of a custom snippet for a Maven build task:

```
"Maven Build Task": {
  "prefix": "mavenbuild",
  "body": [
    "- task: Maven@3",
    "  inputs:",
    "    mavenPomFile: 'pom.xml'",
    "    goals: 'clean install'"
  ],
  "description": "Adds a Maven build task for Spring
Boot"
}
```

Once added, you can simply type mavenbuild in your YAML file and the snippet will expand to the preconfigured Maven build task.

Validating and Testing YAML files

The **YAML** and **Azure Pipelines** extensions help in identifying errors early. Before committing your YAML file to Azure Repos, it's crucial to validate the file to ensure that it follows the correct schema and is free from syntax errors.

Real-time Validation

Both extensions will highlight errors in the YAML file as you type. For instance, if you misspell a task or forget to close a sequence, the error will be displayed immediately with a red underline or warning icon.

Schema-based Validation

The **Azure Pipelines extension** uses schema validation to ensure your YAML files follow the correct format for Azure Pipelines. If any part of your pipeline configuration is invalid, such as missing fields or incorrect data types, it will alert you with detailed messages.

After validating your YAML file, you can test the pipeline locally by using a mock or staging branch in your repository.

With this, we can be assured that these VS Code extensions and features for YAML greatly improves your workflow when working with Azure Pipelines. From real-time validation to schema-based IntelliSense, these tools ensure that your YAML files are correctly structured, error-free, and easy to manage.

Summary

To wrap up this chapter, we looked at Pipeline as Code, specifically how to use Azure Pipelines and YAML to automate and structure CI/CD workflows. We started by learning about the benefits of Pipeline as Code, which allows pipeline configurations to be versioned and integrated with the project's source code. We then created a multi-stage YAML pipeline in which various stages such as development, staging, and production were configured in a single YAML file.

We also included essential VS Code extensions for YAML, such as the YAML and Azure Pipelines extensions for syntax highlighting, validation, and IntelliSense. We also looked at how to manage and validate large YAML files, including features like code folding, outline views, and snippets. In sum, we gained practical experience in automating complicated DevOps workflows in Azure Pipelines with YAML thanks to this chapter.

CHAPTER 3: CONTINUOUS INTEGRATION WITH AZURE PIPELINES

Overview

Continuous Integration (CI) is a practice in which developers regularly integrate their code into a shared repository, resulting in automated builds and tests. In this chapter, we will explore the core concepts of CI and its application through Azure Pipelines. We will start by discussing the importance of CI and how Azure Pipelines can help you streamline this process, especially for Java-based projects like our Spring Boot application. You will learn how to configure build triggers so that the CI pipeline runs automatically whenever there are changes to the codebase, such as commits or pull requests to ensure that the code is constantly tested and rebuilt. On top of that, we will look at how to automate unit testing with testing frameworks like JUnit and Mockito.

This chapter will also introduce static analysis tools for measuring code quality and identifying issues such as bugs, vulnerabilities, and poor coding practices before they reach production. Furthermore, we will use Azure Pipelines to test the Spring Boot project by automating the build, test, and analysis processes, resulting in a dependable and scalable CI environment.

Getting Started with Continuous Integration

CI is a critical DevOps practice that emphasizes frequent integration of code into a shared repository, with automated builds and tests running to catch issues early in the development lifecycle. The goal of CI is to ensure that every change made to the codebase is tested and built automatically, allowing developers to detect and address integration issues as soon as they arise.

In the context of our **Spring Boot** application, Azure Pipelines provides an efficient and automated way to implement CI. Azure Pipelines is a cloud-hosted service that supports multiple languages and frameworks, including Java, making it well-suited for Spring Boot applications. With Azure Pipelines, every time a developer pushes code to a version control system (like Git), the pipeline is triggered to build and test the application. This ensures that the Spring Boot application is always in a buildable state, and any issues introduced by the new code are immediately caught.

The CI process with Azure Pipelines begins by defining a pipeline that contains all the steps needed to build, test, and package the application. For a Spring Boot project, this typically involves pulling the latest changes from the Git repository, running a build process using **Maven** (which handles the project's dependencies), and executing unit tests using frameworks like **JUnit** and **Mockito**. Azure Pipelines then provides detailed logs of each build, helping developers easily track down issues when a build fails.

Configuring Build Triggers

Build triggers are an essential part of CI because they determine when a pipeline will automatically start building and testing your code. With Azure Pipelines, you can configure triggers to automatically kick off the build process when changes are made to your codebase, such as when a new commit is pushed or a pull request is created. In this section, we will dive deeper into configuring **build triggers** for our Spring Boot application using Azure Pipelines.

Understanding Build Triggers

Build triggers in Azure Pipelines help streamline the CI process by automatically initiating builds when certain events occur in your Git repository. These events typically include:

- **Commits**: Every time a developer pushes code to a specific branch, the pipeline is triggered. This is useful for ensuring that every code change is verified through automated tests and builds.
- **Pull Requests**: When a pull request is opened or updated, a pipeline run can be triggered to test the proposed changes before they are merged into the main codebase.

Configuring a Trigger in the YAML Build Pipeline

Referring to the **Spring Boot build pipeline** we created in the previous chapter, we can modify the **azure-pipelines.yml** file to include triggers. These triggers will ensure that the pipeline runs automatically when changes are pushed to the codebase or when pull requests are made.

Following is how you can define a trigger for the **master** branch:

```
trigger:

  - master
```

In this configuration, the **trigger** keyword specifies that the pipeline will run whenever changes are pushed to the **master** branch.

You can also specify multiple branches by listing them under trigger, like this:

```
trigger:

  - master

  - dev
```

This setup ensures that the pipeline is triggered when changes are made to both the **master** and **dev** branches.

Configuring Pull Request Triggers

In addition to triggers for commits, you can also configure **pull request triggers** to automatically test changes before they are merged into the main branch. This is useful for validating code in a feature branch before it is integrated into the **master** branch.

You can add a pull request trigger in the YAML file as follows:

```
pr:

  branches:

    include:

      - master
```

This configuration tells Azure Pipelines to trigger a build when a pull request is opened or updated against the **master** branch. You can also specify other branches if needed, like:

```
pr:

  branches:

    include:

      - master

      - staging
```

With pull request triggers, every time a new commit is added to the feature branch associated with the pull request, the pipeline will automatically build and test the code, providing feedback on whether the new changes pass or fail.

Testing the Build Trigger

To see how build triggers work in action, we will perform the following steps:

- Make a small change to the Spring Boot project code, such as updating a file or adding a comment.
- Commit and push the changes to the **master** branch:

```
git add .
```

```
git commit -m "Updated the Spring Boot application"

git push origin master
```

- Once the push is complete, Azure Pipelines will automatically detect the change and start running the pipeline, triggering a build and test run.
- Then, create a new feature branch and make a change in that branch:

```
git checkout -b feature-branch

git add .

git commit -m "New feature"

git push origin feature-branch
```

- Open a pull request from **feature-branch** to **master** in your Git repository.
- Azure Pipelines will automatically trigger the pipeline to test the changes in the feature branch before merging them into the **master** branch.
- The results of the pipeline (whether it passed or failed) will be visible in the pull request, allowing the team to review the code and ensure it doesn't introduce any issues before merging.

Sometimes, you may want to exclude certain branches from automatic triggers, especially if they are used for temporary or experimental features. For this, you can specify exclusions in your YAML file like this:

```
trigger:

  branches:

    include:

      - master

    exclude:

      - experimental
```

This configuration ensures that builds are triggered on the **master** branch but not on the **experimental** branch. This can be particularly useful in situations where you don't want to run CI on every branch in your repository.

Configuring Path Filters for Triggers

In some cases, you might want to trigger builds only when certain files or directories are modified. For example, if your project contains multiple components, you may only want to run the pipeline when changes are made to the Spring Boot component.

You can configure **path filters** in the YAML file like this:

```yaml
trigger:

  branches:

    include:

      - master

  paths:

    include:

      - src/main/java/**

    exclude:

      - docs/**
```

In the above code snippet,

- The pipeline is triggered when changes are made to any files in the **src/main/java** directory.
- Changes to files in the docs directory will not trigger the pipeline. This allows for more fine-grained control over when pipelines are triggered, ensuring that builds are only run when necessary.

Whether it's a simple code commit or a complex pull request, the pipeline will automatically kick off, ensuring that your application is always in a buildable and testable state. This setup not only improves the efficiency of the CI process but also ensures higher code quality by catching issues early.

Automating Tests in CI pipelines with JUnit and Mockito

JUnit and Mockito Overview

JUnit and **Mockito** are two key libraries that play a critical role in unit testing for Java applications. **JUnit** is a popular testing framework that helps developers write and run tests for individual units of code (such as methods or classes) to ensure they work as expected. On the other hand, **Mockito** is a powerful mocking framework that allows you to simulate the behavior of dependencies, making it easier to test isolated components without needing their actual implementations.

For a Spring Boot application, JUnit is used to test the core logic and functionality of various components, while Mockito is employed to mock services, repositories, or other dependencies, ensuring that the unit tests remain focused on the functionality being tested, without relying on external dependencies like databases or APIs.

Installing and Configuring JUnit and Mockito

Before you can use JUnit and Mockito in your Spring Boot project, you need to include them as dependencies in your Maven **pom.xml** file.

Following are the steps to do that:

- Open your **pom.xml** file and add the following dependencies:

```
<dependencies>

    <!-- JUnit 5 (Jupiter) dependency for testing -->

    <dependency>

        <groupId>org.junit.jupiter</groupId>

        <artifactId>junit-jupiter-api</artifactId>

        <version>5.7.0</version>

        <scope>test</scope>

    </dependency>
```

```
<!-- JUnit 5 Engine -->
<dependency>
    <groupId>org.junit.jupiter</groupId>
    <artifactId>junit-jupiter-engine</artifactId>
    <version>5.7.0</version>
    <scope>test</scope>
</dependency>

<!-- Mockito dependency for mocking -->
<dependency>
    <groupId>org.mockito</groupId>
    <artifactId>mockito-core</artifactId>
    <version>3.6.28</version>
    <scope>test</scope>
</dependency>

<!-- Mockito JUnit 5 integration -->
<dependency>
    <groupId>org.mockito</groupId>
    <artifactId>mockito-junit-jupiter</artifactId>
```

```
        <version>3.6.28</version>

        <scope>test</scope>

    </dependency>

</dependencies>
```

- After adding the dependencies to **pom.xml**, refresh the Maven project in your IDE to download and apply the new dependencies.

Writing Unit Tests with JUnit

Given below is a simple example of how to write a unit test for a service in a Spring Boot application and we will assume you have a **CalculatorService** in the application:

```
public class CalculatorService {

    public int add(int a, int b) {

        return a + b;

    }

}
```

Now, we will create a test case to verify the **add()** method using JUnit.

```
import org.junit.jupiter.api.Test;

import static
org.junit.jupiter.api.Assertions.assertEquals;


public class CalculatorServiceTest {


    @Test
```

```
    public void testAdd() {
        CalculatorService calculatorService = new
CalculatorService();
        int result = calculatorService.add(5, 3);
        assertEquals(8, result, "The addition result
should be 8");
    }
}
```

Here,

- **@Test**: Marks the method as a test case.
- **assertEquals()**: Verifies that the actual result of calculatorService.add(5, 3) is equal to the expected result (8).

You can then run the test.

```
mvn test
```

Maven will compile the project and execute all tests annotated with **@Test**.

Mocking Dependencies with Mockito

In applications, services often rely on other components like repositories or external services. Testing these components in isolation is essential, and that's where **Mockito** comes in. Let us consider we have a UserService that depends on a UserRepository:

```
@Service
public class UserService {
    @Autowired
    private UserRepository userRepository;
```

```
    public User getUserById(Long id) {
        return userRepository.findById(id).orElse(null);
    }
}
```

```
public interface UserRepository extends
JpaRepository<User, Long> { }
```

You can then mock the **UserRepository** to simulate its behavior during testing.

```
import org.junit.jupiter.api.Test;
import org.mockito.InjectMocks;
import org.mockito.Mock;
import org.mockito.Mockito;
import static org.mockito.Mockito.*;
import static org.junit.jupiter.api.Assertions.*;

public class UserServiceTest {

    @Mock
    private UserRepository userRepository;

    @InjectMocks
```

```
    private UserService userService;

    @Test
    public void testGetUserById() {
        // Arrange
        User mockUser = new User(1L, "John Doe");
when(userRepository.findById(1L)).thenReturn(Optional.of(
mockUser));

        // Act
        User user = userService.getUserById(1L);

        // Assert
        assertNotNull(user);
        assertEquals("John Doe", user.getName());
        verify(userRepository).findById(1L);  // Verify
that the method was called
    }
}
```

In the above code snippet,

- **@Mock**: Tells Mockito to create a mock of the **UserRepository**.
- **@InjectMocks**: Automatically injects the mock repository into the **UserService**.

- **when()**: Specifies that when **findById(1L)** is called on the **userRepository**, it should return a mock user.
- **verify()**: Ensures that findById() was called on the mock repository.

Automating Tests in the CI Pipeline

Now that you've written unit tests using JUnit and Mockito, it's time to automate them in your **CI pipeline** using Azure Pipelines. While we do, we will ensure that these tests run every time a new build is triggered.

In your **azure-pipelines.yml** file, add the following Maven task to run tests:

```
pool:
  vmImage: 'ubuntu-latest'

steps:
- task: Maven@3
  inputs:
    mavenPomFile: 'pom.xml'
    goals: 'clean test'

- task: PublishTestResults@2
  inputs:
    testResultsFormat: 'JUnit'
    testResultsFiles: '**/surefire-reports/TEST-*.xml'
    failTaskOnFailedTests: true
```

Once the pipeline is triggered (due to a commit or pull request), Azure Pipelines will automatically run the tests and display the results in the pipeline summary. If all tests pass, the pipeline proceeds to the next stage (e.g., building or deploying).

If tests fail, the pipeline will fail, and you can review the test output in the Azure Pipelines interface.

By utilizing these frameworks, you can validate essential features and simulate dependencies, allowing your unit tests to concentrate on the actions of specific components. Continuous integration (CI) pipeline automation of these tests ensures that your code is continuously tested, which improves code quality and decreases the likelihood of bugs reaching production.

Handling Code Quality with Static Analysis

Static analysis tools are essential in identifying code quality issues, potential bugs, and security vulnerabilities before the code reaches production. These tools assess source code without executing it, allowing developers to detect problems such as bad coding practices, unused variables, or even security vulnerabilities like SQL injection. For Java-based projects like **Spring Boot**, one of the most widely used static analysis tools is **SonarQube**. SonarQube integrates well with Azure Pipelines and provides detailed reports on code quality, security vulnerabilities, and technical debt.

In this section, we will set up **SonarQube** for performing static analysis on our Spring Boot project and configure it to work with our existing CI pipeline in Azure Pipelines.

Setting up SonarQube in Azure Pipelines

Use SonarCloud

SonarQube can be installed locally on your server, or you can use **SonarCloud**, a cloud-hosted version of SonarQube. For now, we will use SonarCloud, which requires no local setup and integrates seamlessly with Azure DevOps.

To sign up for SonarCloud:

- Visit SonarCloud and sign up using your GitHub or Azure DevOps account.
- Once signed up, you can create a new project by importing your Spring Boot project from Azure Repos or GitHub.
- After creating a project in SonarCloud, go to **My Account > Security** and generate a new token. This token will be used to authenticate the Azure Pipeline when running SonarQube analysis.

Install the SonarQube Extension in Azure Pipelines

To integrate SonarQube with Azure Pipelines, you need the **SonarQube extension**:

- Go to the Azure DevOps Marketplace and search for the SonarQube extension.
- Install the extension to your Azure DevOps organization.

This extension provides the necessary tasks to run SonarQube analysis as part of your build pipeline.

Configuring YAML file for SonarQube Analysis

Once the extension is installed, you can modify your existing **azure-pipelines.yml** file to include static analysis with SonarQube.

Update the YAML Pipeline

In your **azure-pipelines.yml** file, you need to add the necessary tasks to run SonarQube analysis during the build phase. Following is how you can configure it:

```
trigger:

  - master


pool:

  vmImage: 'ubuntu-latest'


steps:

  # SonarQube preparation task

  - task: SonarCloudPrepare@1

    inputs:

      SonarCloud: 'SonarCloud'

      organization: 'your-sonarcloud-organization'

      scannerMode: 'CLI'

      configMode: 'manual'
```

```
      projectKey: 'your-project-key'
      organization: 'your-sonarcloud-organization'
      extraProperties: |
        sonar.java.binaries=target/classes

  # Maven build
  - task: Maven@3
    inputs:
      mavenPomFile: 'pom.xml'
      goals: 'clean verify'

  # SonarQube analysis task
  - task: SonarCloudAnalyze@1

  # Publish the analysis results to SonarQube
  - task: SonarCloudPublish@1
    inputs:
      pollingTimeoutSec: '300'
```

In the above configuration script,

- **SonarCloudPrepare@1**: Prepares the SonarQube analysis by specifying the project key, the organization name, and other properties like where the compiled classes are stored.

- **SonarCloudAnalyze@1**: This task performs the actual SonarQube analysis on your project's codebase.
- **SonarCloudPublish@1**: Publishes the analysis results to SonarCloud.

Running Static Analysis in CI Pipeline

After adding SonarQube tasks to your pipeline, the static analysis will automatically run as part of your CI build process every time the pipeline is triggered. For this, after editing the **azure-pipelines.yml** file, push the changes to your repository.

```
git add azure-pipelines.yml

git commit -m "Add SonarQube static analysis"

git push origin master
```

Once the changes are pushed, the pipeline will automatically start running. The SonarQube analysis will be triggered after the Maven build is completed, and the results will be published to SonarCloud.

Viewing the SonarQube Report

After the pipeline finishes running, go to SonarCloud and access your project dashboard. You will see detailed reports on code quality, security vulnerabilities, code smells (potential issues), and technical debt.

The results show,

- **Bugs**: Issues in the code that are likely to cause functional problems, such as null pointer exceptions or array index out-of-bound errors.
- **Vulnerabilities**: Security issues like SQL injections, cross-site scripting (XSS), or sensitive data exposure.
- **Code Smells**: Poor coding practices that don't necessarily cause functional issues but may lead to maintenance difficulties or performance problems in the long run.
- **Technical Debt**: This represents the amount of effort required to fix the code issues identified by SonarQube, helping teams prioritize improvements.

SonarQube also allows you to define **quality gates**, which set thresholds for acceptable code quality. If the quality gate conditions aren't met (e.g., if too many bugs or vulnerabilities are found), the pipeline can fail, preventing poor-quality code from being merged into production.

Once SonarQube is fully integrated into your CI pipeline, it continuously scans your code with every commit or pull request. This means you can catch new bugs or vulnerabilities early, improving the overall quality of the application.

Using Azure Pipelines to Test Project

Now in this final section of this chapter, we will focus on implementing and testing the **CI pipeline** that we've built so far. This will involve running the pipeline to automatically build and test our Spring Boot application whenever changes are made to the codebase. We will also verify that our automated tests, which include unit tests using **JUnit** and **Mockito**, are executed successfully as part of this pipeline.

Ensuring the CI Pipeline is Setup

If you've followed along with the previous sections, you should already have a basic CI pipeline in place that builds the Spring Boot application and runs the unit tests.

Given below is a quick overview of the **azure-pipelines.yml** file that should be in place:

```
trigger:

  - master


pool:

  vmImage: 'ubuntu-latest'


steps:

  # Maven build task

  - task: Maven@3

    inputs:

      mavenPomFile: 'pom.xml'

      goals: 'clean verify'
```

```yaml
  # Publish test results to Azure Pipelines
  - task: PublishTestResults@2
    inputs:
      testResultsFormat: 'JUnit'
      testResultsFiles: '**/surefire-reports/TEST-*.xml'
      failTaskOnFailedTests: true
```

Running the CI Pipeline in Azure Pipelines

Once the pipeline is configured, you can run it to validate the Spring Boot project by following these steps:

Commit and Push Changes to the Repository

Ensure that any changes to your Spring Boot project or the **azure-pipelines.yml** file are committed and pushed to the Git repository.

```
git add .
git commit -m "Trigger CI pipeline for Spring Boot"
git push origin master
```

This will trigger the pipeline, as the **trigger** configuration in the YAML file specifies that any changes to the **master** branch should automatically start the pipeline.

Monitor the Pipeline

After pushing the changes, go to the **Pipelines** section in Azure DevOps to monitor the progress. You will see the pipeline listed, and its current status (in progress, success, or failure) will be displayed in real-time.

Click on the pipeline run to view the details. The pipeline will proceed through the stages of building the application, running tests, and publishing test results.

Viewing Build Logs

Each task within the pipeline provides logs that detail what is happening during the build. If any issues occur during the build or testing phase, you can inspect these logs to identify the root cause.

For example, if the Maven build fails, you will see the error in the build logs. Similarly, if any unit tests fail, the logs will provide detailed output from the JUnit and Mockito tests, helping you debug the issues.

Testing the Spring Boot Project in the Pipeline

During the build process, Maven will execute all the unit tests defined in your Spring Boot project. These tests ensure that the individual components of the application behave as expected. Mockito, which is used to mock dependencies, ensures that the tests remain isolated and focused on specific functionality.

For example, if you've written tests to verify that your **UserService** class behaves correctly, these tests will run as part of the pipeline. If any test fails, the pipeline will fail, and the test results will be shown in the Azure Pipelines dashboard.

Once the tests have run, Azure Pipelines provides a summary of the test results, including:

- Number of tests executed.
- Number of tests passed.
- Number of tests failed.
- Detailed output of each test, including any errors or failures.

The **PublishTestResults@2** task in the pipeline ensures that the results are visible in the **Tests** tab of the pipeline summary. If all tests pass, the pipeline will proceed to the next stage (such as packaging the application or deploying it to a staging environment). If any test fails, the pipeline will stop, ensuring that you don't accidentally merge broken code.

If some tests fail, you can fix the issues in your code, push the changes to the repository, and the pipeline will automatically rerun, verifying that the changes have resolved the issues.

Azure Pipelines provides real-time feedback on build and test results, allowing developers to address issues quickly and maintain a stable codebase. The automated testing process not only validates the functionality of your code but also improves code quality by catching issues early in the development cycle. The entire process—from build triggers to running tests and publishing results—is fully automated, streamlining the CI pipeline and ensuring that the application is always in a buildable, testable, and deployable state.

Summary

As a recap, we covered all the bases when it came to the CI process, including how Azure Pipelines facilitates the automation of code integration, development, and testing. Next, build triggers were configured to ensure that any change in the codebase, whether from a commit or a pull request, automatically initiated the CI pipeline. The pipeline was then enhanced with automated testing via JUnit and Mockito. These frameworks enabled the automation of unit tests, ensuring that individual Spring Boot application units functioned as expected. The tests were set to run automatically during builds by configuring Maven in the CI pipeline. Additionally, the test results were published to Azure Pipelines, providing the team with immediate feedback on any test failures or code issues.

Finally, the chapter discussed the importance of static code analysis using tools such as SonarQube. to perform continuous monitoring of code quality, identifying bugs, code smells, and potential vulnerabilities before the code was deployed. When SonarQube was integrated with the pipeline, all builds were guaranteed to meet the predefined quality standards. As a whole, this chapter stressed the need of automating the complete CI process, from building to testing and quality analysis, to guarantee an efficient and effective development lifecycle.

Chapter 4: Continuous Delivery with Azure Pipelines

Overview

Continuous Delivery ensures that code changes are automatically tested, built, and ready for production with minimal manual intervention. This chapter delves into Continuous Delivery (CD) and how it automated the deployment with Azure Pipelines. We will start by learning about the principles of CD, as well as various deployment strategies like blue-green deployments and canary releases, which help ensure a smooth rollout of new application versions. Next, we will look at deploying Spring Boot applications to Azure. You will learn how to automate the deployment process with Azure Pipelines, allowing each successful build to be deployed directly to a running environment. We will also look at how to manage multiple environments in Azure DevOps, including development, staging, and production.

Furthermore, we will go over the steps to set up Azure Pipelines approval gates and checks. Approval gates allow you to include manual reviews or automated checks between stages, ensuring that code does not go into production until it has been approved by the appropriate stakeholders. Finally, we will look at how to use ARM templates to automate infrastructure provisioning. By the end of this chapter, you will have practical skills to automate deployments, and to manage multiple environments, such that your Spring Boot applications deploy smoothly and reliably.

Understanding Continuous Delivery (CD) and Deployment Strategies

CD has evolved significantly over time, transforming the way software is delivered from development to production environments. In the past, deployment processes were mostly manual, time-consuming, and prone to human errors. However, with the rise of DevOps and tools like Azure DevOps, CD has become automated, allowing for more frequent, reliable, and consistent software releases. The goal of CD is to ensure that code is always in a deployable state and can be safely released to production at any point. Azure DevOps provides a robust platform for CD by automating the steps of building, testing, and deploying applications, enabling organizations to deliver updates to users faster.

Within Azure DevOps, the CD pipeline is tightly integrated with version control, CI pipelines, and testing tools, making it easier to automate and manage releases. Once the CI pipeline has successfully built and tested the code, the CD pipeline ensures that the application is automatically prepared for deployment. Azure DevOps supports a wide range of deployment targets, such as Azure App Service, virtual machines, and Kubernetes clusters, and provides features for managing releases across different environments like development, staging, and production.

Deployment Strategies in Azure DevOps

Azure DevOps also supports various deployment strategies, which are crucial for ensuring smooth and low-risk rollouts. Two popular strategies are **blue-green deployments** and **canary**

releases:

Blue-Green Deployment

This strategy involves maintaining two identical environments, "blue" and "green." While the blue environment runs the current version of the application, the green environment is used to deploy and test the new version. Once the new version is verified, traffic is switched from the blue environment to the green environment, making the switch seamless for users. If any issues arise, traffic can easily be switched back to the blue environment. Azure DevOps facilitates this approach by allowing you to configure different environments and automate the traffic switch using tools like Azure Load Balancer or Traffic Manager.

Canary Release

In a canary release, the new version of the application is deployed to a small subset of users first. This ensures that any potential issues are caught before the full rollout. If the canary version performs well, it is gradually rolled out to more users. Azure DevOps supports canary releases through the use of deployment groups, where you can gradually increase the percentage of users accessing the new version of your application. This method reduces the risk associated with deploying new features by controlling exposure.

Both these deployment strategies, combined with Azure DevOps' ability to integrate with various monitoring and logging tools, allow for safer, more controlled rollouts. They help minimize the risk of deployment failures while ensuring that new versions of applications are delivered to end users smoothly.

Deploying Spring Boot Apps to Azure App Service

Deploying a **Spring Boot** application to **Azure App Service** is a straightforward process that allows you to run your application on a fully managed platform. Azure App Service provides a flexible, scalable environment for hosting web applications and APIs, making it an ideal platform for deploying Java applications, including Spring Boot apps.

Deploying Application to Azure App Service

Preparing Spring Boot Application

Before deploying the Spring Boot application, ensure that it's properly packaged as a deployable artifact, typically a **JAR** or **WAR** file. We can use **Maven** to package the Spring Boot application as below:

- Navigate to the root directory of your Spring Boot project in your terminal.

- Run the following command to package the application:

```
mvn clean package
```

This will generate a **.jar** file in the **target/** directory, which is the artifact that will be deployed to Azure App Service.

Creating Azure App Service Instance

- Go to the Azure Portal and log in to your account.
- Click on **Create a resource** and select **App Service** from the list.
- Fill out the required fields such as the **Subscription**, **Resource Group**, **App Name**, and **Region**.
- For the **Runtime stack**, select **Java 11** (or the version your Spring Boot application is running on).
- For the **Operating System**, choose **Linux** if you prefer a Linux environment, or **Windows** if that's your preference.
- Choose a **Pricing Tier** based on your needs (e.g., B1 or B2 for basic plans or higher tiers for production environments).

After filling in all the details, review the configuration and click **Create**. Azure will take a few moments to provision the new App Service instance.

Deploying Application

Once the App Service is created, navigate to the service.

- In the App Service overview page, go to **Deployment Center**. Here you can select the source from which you want to deploy your application.
- For a manual deployment, you can upload the **.jar** or **.war** file directly.
- For automated deployments, link it to your source control, such as **Azure Repos**, **GitHub**, or **Bitbucket**, where your code is stored.
- Select the appropriate deployment method, and if you are uploading the artifact manually, click **Browse** and upload the **.jar** file from your local system.
- Once uploaded, Azure will automatically deploy and run the application.

After the deployment process completes, you can navigate to the App Service URL to see if the Spring Boot application is running correctly.

Automating Deployment Process using Azure Pipelines

Every time a build is successful, the deployment process is automated and sent to Azure App Service, saving time and effort. After a successful first deployment, we can automate the process by configuring Azure Pipelines in the CI section.

Configure Deployment Stage in YAML Pipeline

To automate the deployment, modify the existing **azure-pipelines.yml** file to include a deployment step. Following is how you can configure the YAML pipeline to deploy the Spring Boot application to Azure App Service:

- Add a new **deployment stage** that deploys the application to Azure App Service after it has been successfully built and tested.

```
trigger:

  - master


pool:

  vmImage: 'ubuntu-latest'


steps:

  # Build and Test steps (already configured in previous
chapters)

  - task: Maven@3

    inputs:

      mavenPomFile: 'pom.xml'

      goals: 'clean verify'


  - task: PublishTestResults@2
```

```
    inputs:
      testResultsFormat: 'JUnit'
      testResultsFiles: '**/surefire-reports/TEST-*.xml'
      failTaskOnFailedTests: true

stages:
  - stage: DeployToAzure
    jobs:
    - deployment: Deploy
      displayName: 'Deploy Spring Boot App to Azure App
Service'
      environment: 'production'
      strategy:
        runOnce:
          deploy:
            steps:
            - task: AzureWebApp@1
              inputs:
                azureSubscription: 'Your Azure
Subscription'
                appName: 'your-app-service-name'
```

```
package:
'$(System.DefaultWorkingDirectory)/target/*.jar'
```

- In your Azure DevOps project, go to **Project Settings > Service connections** and create a new **Azure Resource Manager** service connection.
- Authenticate with your Azure account and select the subscription and App Service you created earlier.
- Once the pipeline is configured with the deployment stage, every time you commit changes to the **master** branch (or other configured branches), the pipeline will:
    - Build the Spring Boot application.
    - Run the automated tests.
    - Deploy the packaged JAR file to the Azure App Service.

Running Automated Deployment Pipeline

Now, push the new changes to the repository.

```
git add .

git commit -m "Updated Spring Boot application"

git push origin master
```

- Go to Azure Pipelines, and you will see the pipeline running through all the configured steps: building, testing, and deploying to Azure App Service.
- Once the pipeline completes successfully, visit your App Service URL to confirm that the new version of the Spring Boot application has been deployed and is running as expected.

This entire process allows for continuous deployment, ensuring that every new build is automatically pushed to the cloud without manual intervention. The integration of Azure Pipelines with Azure App Service provides a seamless, scalable solution for deploying and maintaining Java-based applications, improving the efficiency and reliability of the deployment process.

Managing Multiple Environments in Azure DevOps

Managing multiple environments allows teams to safely deploy code incrementally and troubleshoot any issues in lower environments before reaching end users. In this section, we will explore how to manage multiple environments viz., **development**, **staging**, and **production** within Azure DevOps.

Understanding Environment Management

Azure DevOps allows you to define **environments** within your release pipeline. An environment represents a collection of resources (such as servers or Azure services) where your application is deployed. You typically have different environments for various stages of the deployment process, such as:

- **Development**: Where developers can deploy and test their code during active development.
- **Staging**: A pre-production environment where the code is thoroughly tested with a production-like setup.
- **Production**: The live environment where the final version of the application is deployed for end users.

In Azure Pipelines, environments are linked to different stages, and each stage contains specific jobs and tasks for that environment. This structure allows for automated deployment to multiple environments in sequence, ensuring that the code passes through all necessary testing gates.

Setting up Multiple Environments in YAML file

Now, we will extend the **azure-pipelines.yml** file to deploy the Spring Boot application to three different environments. Each environment will have its own deployment stage, allowing you to deploy, test, and validate the application in each one.

Given below is how you can structure your YAML pipeline to manage multiple environments:

```
trigger:

  - master



pool:

  vmImage: 'ubuntu-latest'
```

```yaml
steps:
  # Build and Test Steps
  - task: Maven@3
    inputs:
      mavenPomFile: 'pom.xml'
      goals: 'clean verify'

  - task: PublishTestResults@2
    inputs:
      testResultsFormat: 'JUnit'
      testResultsFiles: '**/surefire-reports/TEST-*.xml'
      failTaskOnFailedTests: true

# Define the stages for different environments

stages:
  # Development environment
  - stage: DeployToDev
    jobs:
    - deployment: DeployToDevelopment
      displayName: 'Deploy to Development'
```

```
      environment: 'Development'
      strategy:
        runOnce:
          deploy:
            steps:
            - task: AzureWebApp@1
              inputs:
                azureSubscription: 'Your Azure
Subscription'
                appName: 'spring-boot-dev'
                package:
'$(System.DefaultWorkingDirectory)/target/*.jar'

  # Staging environment
  - stage: DeployToStaging
    dependsOn: DeployToDev
    condition: succeeded()
    jobs:
    - deployment: DeployToStaging
      displayName: 'Deploy to Staging'
      environment: 'Staging'
      strategy:
```

```
        runOnce:
          deploy:
            steps:
            - task: AzureWebApp@1
              inputs:
                azureSubscription: 'Your Azure
Subscription'
                appName: 'spring-boot-staging'
                package:
'$(System.DefaultWorkingDirectory)/target/*.jar'

  # Production environment
  - stage: DeployToProduction
    dependsOn: DeployToStaging
    condition: succeeded()
    jobs:
    - deployment: DeployToProduction
      displayName: 'Deploy to Production'
      environment: 'Production'
      strategy:
        runOnce:
          deploy:
```

```
            steps:

            - task: AzureWebApp@1

              inputs:

                azureSubscription: 'Your Azure
Subscription'

                appName: 'spring-boot-prod'

                package:
'$(System.DefaultWorkingDirectory)/target/*.jar'
```

Each of the stages defined in the above script uses the **AzureWebApp@1** task to deploy the packaged Spring Boot application (JAR file) to its corresponding Azure App Service.

Linking Environments in Azure DevOps

In Azure DevOps, environments are linked to the **Azure Resource Manager** services (such as App Service, Kubernetes clusters, or virtual machines) where the application will be deployed.

To define environments manually,

- Go to your **Pipelines > Environments** in Azure DevOps, and create **Development**, **Staging**, and **Production** environments.
- You can set up additional rules, approval gates, and permissions for these environments, ensuring that deployments to production are safeguarded by approvals.
- To make the pipeline more flexible, you can define different environment-specific variables like database connection strings, APIs, and resource configurations using Azure Pipelines' **variables** feature.

For example:

```
variables:

  devAppName: 'spring-boot-dev'

  stagingAppName: 'spring-boot-staging'

  prodAppName: 'spring-boot-prod'
```

```
stages:
  - stage: DeployToDev
    jobs:
    - deployment: DeployToDevelopment
      environment: 'Development'
      steps:
      - task: AzureWebApp@1
        inputs:
          appName: '$(devAppName)'
          ...
```

This approach centralizes configuration and prevents hardcoding values within the pipeline, making it easier to manage and maintain.

Setting Deployment Conditions

Azure DevOps allows you to set conditions on stages and jobs to control when certain deployments should occur. For example, you might want to ensure that production deployments only happen after a manual approval or after passing certain checks in the staging environment.

Conditional Deployment

Use the **condition** field to set conditions for deployments. For instance, production deployments should only happen if the staging deployment is successful:

```
condition: succeeded()
```

Approvals and Gates

You can configure approval gates for sensitive environments like production. Before deploying to production, a manual review process can be enforced in Azure DevOps.

To configure this:

- Go to Pipelines > Environments in Azure DevOps.
- Select the **Production** environment and set up **Approvals and Checks**.
- Define a list of reviewers who must approve the deployment before it proceeds to production.

Triggering Pipeline and Managing Environment Flow

Once the environments are configured in the pipeline, the deployment flow can be triggered automatically by a push or pull request to the main branch.

The pipeline will:

- Deploy to the **development** environment first.
- If the deployment is successful, it will move to the **staging** environment.
- After testing in staging, the deployment proceeds to the **production** environment, ensuring that each environment is validated before moving to the next.

Each of gthe above deployed environment serves a specific purpose, and Azure Pipelines provides robust tools for automating the deployment process, safeguarding production environments with conditional checks and approval gates, and managing environment-specific configurations effectively. This process leads to more reliable and consistent deployments, minimizing risk and increasing confidence in the software release process.

Implementing Approval Gates and Checks

Approval gates ensure that the deployment to specific environments, such as staging or production, doesn't proceed automatically without manual validation or certain checks passing. In this section, we will implement **approval gates and checks** within Azure Pipelines for our Spring Boot application. This is especially useful in production environments where deploying without approval could have significant consequences.

Setting up Environments for Approvals

Before configuring approval gates, you need to ensure that your **environments** (development, staging, production) are set up in **Azure DevOps**. Following are the steps to configure environments for approval gates:

- In your Azure DevOps project, go to **Pipelines > Environments**.

- You will see a list of environments if they are already created. If not, create environments for **development**, **staging**, and **production**.
- Click on the environment (for instance, **Production**) where you want to implement approval gates.
- In the environment settings, you will see the **Approvals and Checks** option. Click on **+ Add** to configure approvals.
- Choose **Approvals** from the available options.
- Add the approvers, who can be individuals or groups, responsible for reviewing and approving deployments. You can also set the timeout period (e.g., 1 hour or 24 hours) within which the approval needs to be provided.

Adding Approval Gates in the YAML Pipeline

To implement approval gates in the **YAML pipeline**, the stages that require approval must be configured to wait for approval before proceeding. Following are the steps to configure it in the **azure-pipelines.yml** file:

- Modify the YAML Pipeline

Following is an updated version of the **azure-pipelines.yml** file that includes approval gates for the **Production** stage:

```
trigger:

  - master


pool:

  vmImage: 'ubuntu-latest'


stages:

  - stage: DeployToDev

    jobs:

    - deployment: DeployToDevelopment
```

```
      displayName: 'Deploy to Development'
      environment: 'Development'
      strategy:
        runOnce:
          deploy:
            steps:
            - task: AzureWebApp@1
              inputs:
                azureSubscription: 'Your Azure
Subscription'
                appName: 'spring-boot-dev'
                package:
'$(System.DefaultWorkingDirectory)/target/*.jar'

  - stage: DeployToStaging
    dependsOn: DeployToDev
    condition: succeeded()
    jobs:
    - deployment: DeployToStaging
      displayName: 'Deploy to Staging'
      environment: 'Staging'
      strategy:
```

```
        runOnce:
          deploy:
            steps:
            - task: AzureWebApp@1
              inputs:
                azureSubscription: 'Your Azure
Subscription'
                appName: 'spring-boot-staging'
                package:
'$(System.DefaultWorkingDirectory)/target/*.jar'

  - stage: DeployToProduction
    dependsOn: DeployToStaging
    condition: succeeded()
    jobs:
    - deployment: DeployToProduction
      displayName: 'Deploy to Production'
      environment: 'Production'
      strategy:
        runOnce:
          deploy:
            steps:
```

```
            - task: AzureWebApp@1
              inputs:
                azureSubscription: 'Your Azure 
Subscription'
                appName: 'spring-boot-prod'
                package: 
'$(System.DefaultWorkingDirectory)/target/*.jar'
```

The **Production** environment requires manual approval before the pipeline proceeds with deployment to production.

- Approval Configuration in YAML

The environment settings (in the Azure DevOps UI) dictate when the approval step kicks in. If you've configured an **approval gate** for the **Production** environment as shown in Step 1, then after the pipeline reaches the Production stage, it will automatically pause and await manual approval from the configured users or groups.

Once approval is given, the pipeline will continue deploying the application to production.

Testing Approval Gates in Action

We will test the approval process by triggering the pipeline and watching how the approval gates work. Now, to trigger the Pipeline, make a minor change to the Spring Boot code or pipeline file and push the changes to the **master** branch:

```
git add .
git commit -m "Testing approval gates"
git push origin master
```

Then, to monitor the Pipeline,

- Go to the **Pipelines** section in Azure DevOps to monitor the pipeline's progress. It will deploy to the **Development** and **Staging** environments first.
- When the pipeline reaches the **Production** environment, it will stop and await approval.

- The pipeline will show as **Pending approval** in the Production stage.
- An email notification will be sent to the approvers you configured earlier.
- Approvers can navigate to the **Pipelines** page in Azure DevOps, click on the pipeline, and manually approve the deployment. Alternatively, if needed, the approver can reject the deployment.
- Once approval is granted, the pipeline will resume and complete the deployment to production.

Implementing Additional Checks

Besides manual approval gates, Azure Pipelines allows you to add **automated checks** like **business hours deployment checks**, **custom script validations**, or **monitoring tool checks**. These checks ensure that the application can only be deployed under specific conditions.

For example, you may only want to deploy during working hours, or you may need to ensure certain health checks are in place before deployment proceeds.

For example, adding Business Hours check:

- In the **Approvals and Checks** settings of the environment, you can add a **Business Hours Check** to restrict deployments to specific time windows (e.g., only between 9 AM to 5 PM on weekdays).
- Add a new check by clicking on **+ Add** and selecting **Business Hours**.
- Define the hours during which deployments are allowed to this environment.

And, for adding Health check:

- You can configure **Health Checks** to ensure that the services or infrastructure that the application depends on are healthy before proceeding with deployment.
- Add a **Health Check** by navigating to the **Approvals and Checks** section of the environment settings and selecting the **Health Check** option. You can configure the health endpoint URL that Azure will check before deployment.

This entire setup helps teams maintain a secure and reliable deployment process, reducing the risk of errors or unplanned downtime in production environments.

Using ARM Templates to Automate Infrastructure Provisioning

ARM templates provide a declarative way to define and deploy resources in Azure, ensuring that the infrastructure is provisioned consistently and automatically as part of your CD pipeline. By integrating ARM templates into the deployment pipeline, you can automate the provisioning of necessary infrastructure, such as App Service instances, databases, and networking components, ensuring that the environments are properly configured before application deployment. Here, we will explore how to use **ARM templates** to automate infrastructure provisioning for our Spring Boot application.

Understanding ARM Templates

A typical ARM template consists of the following sections:

- **Resources**: Defines the Azure resources (e.g., App Service, Database, Virtual Network).
- **Parameters**: Input values that can be customized during deployment (e.g., App Service name, region).
- **Variables**: Reusable values that are computed during the deployment.
- **Outputs**: Return values that are exposed after deployment (e.g., App Service URL).

Creating ARM Template for Spring Boot Infrastructure

We will create an ARM template that provisions the infrastructure required for our Spring Boot application. This template will create an **Azure App Service** and an **App Service Plan** (the compute resource that hosts the App Service).

Create a JSON File

Start by creating a new file called **azuredeploy.json** in the root directory of your project. Then, define the ARM Template. Given below is a basic ARM template that provisions an App Service Plan and an App Service:

```
{
  "$schema":
"https://schema.management.azure.com/schemas/2019-04-
01/deploymentTemplate.json#",
  "contentVersion": "1.0.0.0",
  "parameters": {
    "appServicePlanName": {
```

```
      "type": "string",
      "defaultValue": "AppServicePlan"
    },
    "webAppName": {
      "type": "string",
      "defaultValue": "spring-boot-app"
    },
    "location": {
      "type": "string",
      "defaultValue": "[resourceGroup().location]"
    },
    "skuName": {
      "type": "string",
      "defaultValue": "B1"
    }
  },
  "resources": [
    {
      "type": "Microsoft.Web/serverfarms",
      "apiVersion": "2021-01-15",
      "name": "[parameters('appServicePlanName')]",
```

```
      "location": "[parameters('location')]",
      "sku": {
        "name": "[parameters('skuName')]",
        "tier": "Basic",
        "size": "B1",
        "family": "B",
        "capacity": 1
      },
      "properties": {
        "reserved": true
      }
    },
    {
      "type": "Microsoft.Web/sites",
      "apiVersion": "2021-01-15",
      "name": "[parameters('webAppName')]",
      "location": "[parameters('location')]",
      "properties": {
        "serverFarmId":
"[resourceId('Microsoft.Web/serverfarms',
parameters('appServicePlanName'))]"
      },
```

```
        "dependsOn": [
          "[resourceId('Microsoft.Web/serverfarms',
parameters('appServicePlanName'))]"
        ]
      }
    ],
    "outputs": {
      "webAppUri": {
        "type": "string",
        "value": "[concat('https://',
parameters('webAppName'), '.azurewebsites.net')]"
      }
    }
}
```

In the above ARM Template,

- **Parameters**: Defines inputs like the App Service Plan name, App Service name, region, and SKU (pricing tier).
- **Resources**: Creates an App Service Plan and an App Service.
- **Outputs**: Returns the URL of the deployed App Service.

Then, save the template.

Deploying the ARM Template Using Azure CLI

Next, you can deploy the ARM template manually or automate it in the pipeline. First, we will deploy it manually using **Azure CLI** to ensure everything works as expected. To do this,

- Open Azure CLI and log in.

```
az login
```

- Create a Resource Group (if you don't have one).

```
az group create --name MyResourceGroup --location eastus
```

- Use the following command to deploy the ARM template. This will deploy the App Service and App Service Plan based on the parameters defined in the template.

```
az deployment group create \

  --resource-group MyResourceGroup \

  --template-file azuredeploy.json \

  --parameters appServicePlanName=AppServicePlan
webAppName=spring-boot-app
```

- Once the deployment completes, you can verify it in the Azure Portal by navigating to the **Resource Group** and checking the newly created resources.
- Use the **Outputs** section of the ARM template to find the deployed App Service URL.

Automating ARM Template Deployment

To automate the deployment of the infrastructure using the ARM template within your Azure Pipelines, we need to add a new stage in our pipeline that deploys the resources before the application is deployed.

For this, add a new step that uses the AzureResourceManagerTemplateDeployment@3 task to deploy the ARM template:

```
stages:

  # Infrastructure provisioning stage

  - stage: ProvisionInfrastructure

    displayName: 'Provision Infrastructure with ARM
Template'
```

```
    jobs:
    - job: DeployInfrastructure
      steps:
      - task: AzureResourceManagerTemplateDeployment@3
        inputs:
          deploymentScope: 'Resource Group'
          azureResourceManagerConnection: 'Your Azure
Subscription'
          subscriptionId: 'YOUR_SUBSCRIPTION_ID'
          action: 'Create Or Update Resource Group'
          resourceGroupName: 'MyResourceGroup'
          location: 'East US'
          templateLocation: 'Linked artifact'
          csmFile: 'azuredeploy.json'
          csmParametersFile: ''
          overrideParameters: '-appServicePlanName
AppServicePlan -webAppName spring-boot-app'
```

After this, push changes to the repository to trigger the pipeline, and the new **ProvisionInfrastructure** stage will be executed. This stage will deploy the required infrastructure before the application deployment.

Once the infrastructure is provisioned, the pipeline will proceed with deploying the Spring Boot application to the newly created App Service.

ARM templates ensure that all environments (development, staging, production) are provisioned consistently, minimizing the risk of manual configuration errors. This approach also streamlines the process of managing and scaling infrastructure in Azure, allowing you to manage both your application and infrastructure as code, and thereby making deployments more reliable and repeatable.

Summary

In conclusion, this chapter covered the fundamentals of CD and how to put Azure Pipelines into practice. We first looked at how CD has evolved into an automated, dependable process within Azure DevOps, allowing for more frequent and controlled software releases. Several deployment strategies were discussed, including blue-green deployments and canary releases, which enable smooth, low-risk application rollouts across environments. We then proceeded to deploy a Spring Boot application to Azure App Service, automating the process with Azure Pipelines. The chapter also covered managing multiple environments (development, staging, and production), demonstrating how Azure DevOps makes it simple to configure and deploy to different environments sequentially while protecting the production environment through validation checks.

Another important aspect of the chapter was implementing approval gates and checks to prevent critical environments from being updated without proper validation. Finally, we explored the use of ARM templates to automate infrastructure provisioning, ensuring that all required infrastructure (such as App Service Plans and Web Apps) is provisioned as part of the deployment pipeline.

CHAPTER 5: MANAGING DEPENDENCIES WITH AZURE ARTIFACTS

Overview

We are now going to start with the second section of this book, which is Chapter 5. In this chapter, we go into dependency management with Azure Artifacts. Azure Artifacts is a package management tool that helps you create, host, and share packages with your team. This chapter will walk you through the process of getting started with Azure Artifacts, including creating and configuring Maven or NuGet feeds for your project. By managing dependencies in Azure Artifacts, you can simplify the process of sharing and reusing libraries across multiple projects while keeping the environment secure and controlled.

You will also learn how to incorporate these dependencies into your CI/CD pipeline so that the builds always pull the correct package versions and that any updates to these dependencies are handled efficiently. Next, you will learn how to apply version control to packages to easily manage multiple versions of a package in different environments and to easily roll back to previous versions. Last but not least, this chapter will show you how to publish artifacts from build pipelines, so you can make updated library or application package versions and distribute them through Azure Artifacts.

Getting Started with Azure Artifacts

Azure Artifacts is a fully integrated package management solution in **Azure DevOps** that allows teams to create, share, and consume packages across projects. It supports multiple package types such as **Maven**, **NuGet**, **npm**, and **Python**, making it ideal for managing dependencies in modern software development. By using Azure Artifacts, you can ensure that all your projects have access to the right versions of external libraries and internal packages, streamlining the development process while maintaining strict control over versioning.

In this section, we will walk through setting up **Azure Artifacts** in our existing environment, making it ready to be used for managing dependencies in our **Spring Boot application**. Spring Boot primarily uses **Maven** for dependency management, so we will focus on setting up Maven feeds in Azure Artifacts to store and share Java packages.

Creating an Azure Artifacts Feed

A feed acts as a central repository from which packages are pushed and consumed. Before integrating Azure Artifacts into our pipeline, we first need to create a **feed** where we can store and manage our packages.

Navigate to Azure Artifacts

- Go to your **Azure DevOps** project.
- From the left-hand menu, select **Artifacts**.

Create a New Feed

- Click on **+ New feed**.
- Provide a name for the feed (e.g., **SpringBootDependencies**).
- Set the visibility of the feed. You can make it public (accessible to everyone) or private (only accessible to specific teams or projects).
- For this project, select **private** to ensure that only authorized members of the team can access the packages.
- Click **Create** to set up the feed.

Configure Permissions

- You can configure who has access to the feed by navigating to the **Permissions** tab.
- Add contributors, readers, or admins, depending on their roles in managing or consuming packages.

Maven for Azure Artifacts

Next, we need to configure Maven to push and pull dependencies from the feed we just created.

Connect to Feed

- In the **Azure Artifacts** feed page, you will find an option to **Connect to feed**. Click on it, and select **Maven** from the list of available package types.
- You will see instructions to update your Maven configuration, including the **settings.xml** file that tells Maven where to find and store dependencies.

Update Maven Settings

- Open the settings.xml file (~/.m2/settings.xml).
- Then, add the following configuration to the servers and mirrors sections of the settings.xml file:

```
<servers>

  <server>

    <id>your-artifacts-feed</id>
```

```
    <username>Azure DevOps Personal Access Token
(PAT)</username>

    <password>YourPATToken</password>

  </server>

</servers>


<mirrors>

  <mirror>

    <id>artifacts-feed-mirror</id>

    <mirrorOf>*</mirrorOf>

<url>https://pkgs.dev.azure.com/yourorganization/_packagi
ng/your-feed/maven/v1</url>

  </mirror>

</mirrors>
```

- Replace **your-artifacts-feed** and **your-feed** with the values from your Azure Artifacts feed.
- Generate a **Personal Access Token (PAT)** in Azure DevOps by going to **User settings > Personal Access Tokens**.

Configure Project's POM File

Update your Spring Boot project's **pom.xml** file to include the new repository for dependencies.

```
<repositories>

  <repository>
```

```
    <id>your-artifacts-feed</id>

<url>https://pkgs.dev.azure.com/yourorganization/_packagi
ng/your-feed/maven/v1</url>
  </repository>
</repositories>

<distributionManagement>
  <repository>
    <id>your-artifacts-feed</id>

<url>https://pkgs.dev.azure.com/yourorganization/_packagi
ng/your-feed/maven/v1</url>
  </repository>
</distributionManagement>
```

This configuration allows your Maven project to download dependencies from the Azure Artifacts feed and push any custom packages back to the feed.

Uploading and Consuming Packages

Once you have created your Maven, you can publish it to Azure Artifacts using the following command:

```
mvn deploy
```

This will push your package to the feed configured in the **pom.xml** file.

Next, to consume packages stored in the Azure Artifacts feed, simply add the required dependency in your **pom.xml** file as usual, and Maven will fetch it from the Azure feed:

```
<dependency>
  <groupId>com.yourcompany</groupId>
  <artifactId>your-package</artifactId>
  <version>1.0.0</version>
</dependency>
```

Azure Artifacts will ensure that the package is downloaded from the specified feed.

Integrating Azure Artifacts with CI/CD Pipeline

Now that Azure Artifacts is set up, the final step is to integrate it into your **CI/CD pipeline**.

In your **azure-pipelines.yml** file, ensure that the Maven build process uses the correct feed to download dependencies. Given below is an example configuration:

```
trigger:
  - master


pool:
  vmImage: 'ubuntu-latest'


steps:
- task: Maven@3
  inputs:
    mavenPomFile: 'pom.xml'
    goals: 'clean install'
```

```
    options: '--settings
$(System.DefaultWorkingDirectory)/settings.xml'
```

After building the package, you can also publish it to Azure Artifacts as part of the pipeline:

```
- task: Maven@3

  inputs:

    mavenPomFile: 'pom.xml'

    goals: 'deploy'

    options: '--settings
$(System.DefaultWorkingDirectory)/settings.xml'
```

This will automatically push the built package to the Azure Artifacts feed.

In short, we explored to get started with **Azure Artifacts** by creating a feed, configuring Maven for dependency management, and integrating it into our Spring Boot project. We also uploaded and consumed packages from the feed and integrated the feed into our CI/CD pipeline.

Setting up NuGet Feeds

NuGet is a popular package management tool primarily used in .NET development, but it can also be integrated into other environments for managing and sharing reusable libraries. Although Spring Boot applications typically rely on **Maven** for dependency management, there are scenarios where you might want to use **NuGet** for shared libraries or work with .NET components in a microservices architecture.

Let us learn how to do it.

Creating a NuGet Feed in Azure Artifacts

To set up a **NuGet feed** in Azure Artifacts,

- Go to your **Azure DevOps** project and select **Artifacts** from the left-hand menu.
- Click on **+ New feed**.
- Provide a name for the feed (e.g., **SpringBootNuGetFeed**) and set the feed's visibility to **private** or **public** depending on your requirements.

- Click **Create** to set up the feed. This feed will be used to store and share NuGet packages.
- In the **Permissions** tab, configure who can access the feed.

For internal team collaboration, you can limit access to authorized users or groups. You can also grant **read** or **contribute** permissions as needed.

Setting up NuGet on Your Local Machine

Once the NuGet feed is created, you will need to configure your development environment to connect to it. You can do it in this way:

- Download the **NuGet CLI** from the official NuGet website, and then use NuGet from the command line to push or pull packages.
- In the Azure DevOps **Artifacts** page, select **Connect to Feed** and choose **NuGet** as the package type.
- The page will provide you with instructions for configuring **Visual Studio** or **NuGet CLI** to work with the feed.
- Open Visual Studio and go to Tools > NuGet Package Manager > Package Manager Settings.
- Under the **Package Sources** section, click **Add** and enter the following details:
    - **Name**: SpringBootNuGetFeed
    - **Source**: The NuGet feed URL from Azure Artifacts
- Click **OK** to save the configuration.

Pushing NuGet Package to Azure Artifacts

We will create a NuGet package and push it to the feed we created in Azure Artifacts. This package could be a reusable component, utility library, or other code that multiple projects (including Spring Boot) might consume.

- Create a NuGet Package

Suppose you have a reusable .NET library project. To create a NuGet package from this project:

```
nuget pack MyLibrary.csproj
```

This will generate a **.nupkg** file, which is the NuGet package.

- Push the Package to Azure Artifacts

Use the **NuGet CLI** to push the package to the Azure Artifacts NuGet feed:

```
nuget push MyLibrary.nupkg -Source
https://pkgs.dev.azure.com/yourorganization/_packaging/Sp
ringBootNuGetFeed/nuget/v3/index.json -ApiKey <API_KEY>
```

Replace <API_KEY> with a placeholder value such as AzureArtifacts. Azure Artifacts uses the feed URL for authentication, so the API key is a dummy value here.

Consuming NuGet Packages in Other Projects

Once your NuGet package is pushed to Azure Artifacts, it can be reused across multiple projects, including .NET services or Spring Boot applications where you need a common library.

Now, to use the NuGet package in another .NET project, configure the **NuGet.config** file or use Visual Studio to reference the feed. To do this,

- In the other project, run the following command to install the package from the Azure Artifacts feed:

```
nuget install MyLibrary -Source SpringBootNuGetFeed
```

- Alternatively, use **Visual Studio** to search for and install the package via the **NuGet Package Manager**.

If your Spring Boot project needs to consume the library as a dependency, you can package the .NET library as a **JAR** and upload it to the **Maven** repository or convert it into a shared service that can be accessed via REST APIs.

Integrating NuGet Packages into CI/CD Pipeline

To automate the management and consumption of NuGet packages, you can integrate NuGet feeds into your **CI/CD pipeline**. To do this,

- In your **azure-pipelines.yml** file, add a step to restore NuGet packages from Azure Artifacts during the build process.

```
steps:

- task: NuGetCommand@2

  inputs:

    command: 'restore'
```

```
    feedsToUse: 'select'

    vstsFeed: 'yourorganization/SpringBootNuGetFeed'
```

- This above step restores all NuGet packages from the configured feed during the build.
- If your pipeline produces new versions of shared libraries, you can publish them to Azure Artifacts automatically using the **NuGetCommand** task as below:

```
steps:

- task: NuGetCommand@2

  inputs:

    command: 'push'

    packagesToPush:
'$(Build.ArtifactStagingDirectory)/*.nupkg'

    nuGetFeedType: 'internal'

    publishVstsFeed:
'yourorganization/SpringBootNuGetFeed'
```

This above configuration automatically pushes the newly built packages to the NuGet feed for future use in other projects.

Integrating Dependencies into CI/CD Pipeline

In this section, we will focus on **integrating dependencies** into the CI/CD pipeline, specifically for the **Spring Boot project** that we have been building. We will demonstrate how to configure **Azure Pipelines** to automatically restore and use dependencies from **Azure Artifacts** as part of the build process. If we do this, the pipeline will handle dependency management seamlessly, without manual intervention.

Integrating Maven Dependencies into CI/CD Pipeline

We will first ensure that the **Maven dependencies** for our Spring Boot project are integrated into the CI/CD pipeline. To do this,

- Open the **pom.xml** file of your Spring Boot project.
- Ensure that the **repository** for Azure Artifacts is added so Maven knows where to pull the dependencies from.

```
<repositories>

  <repository>

    <id>your-artifacts-feed</id>


<url>https://pkgs.dev.azure.com/yourorganization/_packagi
ng/your-feed/maven/v1</url>

  </repository>

</repositories>
```

- Replace **your-feed** and **yourorganization** with the actual values for your project.
- We now need to modify the CI/CD pipeline YAML file to ensure Maven dependencies are restored as part of the build process.

Given below is how the pipeline file should be structured to restore dependencies and build the Spring Boot project:

```
trigger:

  - master


pool:

  vmImage: 'ubuntu-latest'


steps:

- task: Maven@3
```

```
  inputs:
    mavenPomFile: 'pom.xml'
    goals: 'clean install'
    options: '--settings
$(System.DefaultWorkingDirectory)/settings.xml'


- task: PublishTestResults@2
  inputs:
    testResultsFormat: 'JUnit'
    testResultsFiles: '**/surefire-reports/TEST-*.xml'
    failTaskOnFailedTests: true
```

Next, push changes to your repository to trigger the pipeline:

```
git add .
git commit -m "Integrated Maven dependencies in CI
pipeline"
git push origin master
```

Maven will pull the dependencies from the Azure Artifacts feed. The project will be compiled and built. Then, unit tests will be executed, and results will be published to Azure DevOps.

Integrating NuGet Dependencies into CI/CD Pipeline

Similar to Maven, we can configure the pipeline to restore NuGet dependencies in a similar manner as below:

- Configure the **NuGet.config** file in your project to reference the Azure Artifacts feed.

```
<configuration>
```

```
  <packageSources>
    <add key="AzureArtifacts"
value="https://pkgs.dev.azure.com/yourorganization/_packa
ging/your-feed/nuget/v3/index.json" />
  </packageSources>
</configuration>
```

- Replace **your-feed** and **yourorganization** with the correct values.
- Update the pipeline YAML file to include a step that restores and uses NuGet packages from Azure Artifacts.

```
trigger:
  - master

pool:
  vmImage: 'windows-latest'

steps:
- task: NuGetCommand@2
  inputs:
    command: 'restore'
    feedsToUse: 'select'
    vstsFeed: 'yourorganization/SpringBootNuGetFeed'
```

```yaml
- task: VSBuild@1
  inputs:
    solution: '**/*.sln'

- task: PublishTestResults@2
  inputs:
    testResultsFormat: 'VSTest'
    testResultsFiles: '**/TestResults/*.trx'
```

After setting up the NuGet feed and updating the pipeline YAML file, push your changes to the repository to trigger the pipeline.

```
git add .

git commit -m "Integrated NuGet dependencies in CI pipeline"

git push origin master
```

The Azure Pipelines will,

- Restore the NuGet dependencies from Azure Artifacts.
- Build the project.
- Run unit tests and publish the test results.

Managing Version Control for Dependencies

In both Maven and NuGet setups, version control plays an important role in ensuring stability in the CI/CD pipeline. By specifying exact versions of dependencies, you ensure that your project always uses the correct versions during builds and tests.

To do this,

- In the **pom.xml** file, specify versions for each dependency:

```xml
<dependency>
   <groupId>com.yourcompany</groupId>
   <artifactId>your-shared-library</artifactId>
   <version>1.0.0</version>
</dependency>
```

- In .NET projects, specify package versions in the **packages.config** or **csproj** files:

```xml
<PackageReference Include="Your.Shared.Library"
Version="1.0.0" />
```

This whole thing ensures consistency across different environments and avoids compatibility issues when newer versions of dependencies are released.

Integrating dependencies into the **CI/CD pipeline** is essential for ensuring that your Spring Boot project (or any other project) builds consistently across environments. This setup not only simplifies dependency management but also ensures stability by controlling the versions of packages used in the build process.

Managing Version Control for Packages

In this section, we will focus on **managing version control for packages** that have been integrated into our CI/CD pipeline using **Azure Artifacts**. We will also demonstrate how to roll back to previous versions of packages if needed.

Managing Package Versions in Maven

Managing versions of these dependencies is a straightforward process. By specifying an exact version number for each dependency, you can ensure that your application uses the intended version of each library, avoiding unexpected changes when new versions are released.

Setting Package Versions

- Open the **pom.xml** file of your Spring Boot project.
- To specify the version of a dependency, include the **version** tag within the dependency declaration:

```xml
<dependency>

  <groupId>com.yourcompany</groupId>

  <artifactId>your-shared-library</artifactId>

  <version>1.0.0</version>

</dependency>
```

This ensures that version **1.0.0** of the **your-shared-library** is used in the project.

Upgrading to a New Version

- If a new version of the dependency is available (e.g., 1.1.0), you can simply update the version in the pom.xml file:

```xml
<dependency>

  <groupId>com.yourcompany</groupId>

  <artifactId>your-shared-library</artifactId>

  <version>1.1.0</version>

</dependency>
```

- Commit the change to your repository, and the CI pipeline will automatically pick up the new version during the next build.

Rolling Back to a Previous Version

If an issue is detected with the new version, you can easily roll back by reverting the version number in the **pom.xml** file to the previous stable version:

```xml
<dependency>

  <groupId>com.yourcompany</groupId>

  <artifactId>your-shared-library</artifactId>

  <version>1.0.0</version>
```

```
</dependency>
```

After pushing the change to the repository, the CI pipeline will revert to using version 1.0.0 of the package during the next build.

Maven also allows specifying version ranges if you want more flexibility with versions. For example, you can use a range to accept any patch-level updates:

```
<version>[1.0.0,1.1.0)</version>
```

This range includes any version starting from **1.0.0** up to, but not including, **1.1.0**. This can be useful when you want minor updates but want to avoid major version changes.

Managing NuGet Package Versions

If your project uses **NuGet** for managing dependencies, you will handle version control through the **packages.config** file or the project's **csproj** file.

Setting Package Versions in NuGet

For each dependency, you specify the exact version of the NuGet package. In the **csproj** file, it will look like this:

```
<PackageReference Include="Your.Shared.Library"
Version="1.0.0" />
```

Upgrading to a New Version

If a new version of the package is available, simply change the version number:

```
<PackageReference Include="Your.Shared.Library"
Version="1.1.0" />
```

After committing the change, the pipeline will pick up the new version.

Rolling Back to a Previous Version

If you need to roll back to a previous version, revert the version in the **csproj** or **packages.config** file to the last known stable version:

```
<PackageReference Include="Your.Shared.Library"
Version="1.0.0" />
```

Using Version Ranges in NuGet

NuGet also allows you to define version ranges for dependencies, giving more flexibility to manage minor updates:

```
<PackageReference Include="Your.Shared.Library"
Version="[1.0.0,1.1.0)" />
```

This range will include all versions starting from **1.0.0** up to, but not including, **1.1.0**.

Version Control and Package Publishing in CI/CD Pipeline

After updating and building your project in the CI/CD pipeline, you can publish the new version of the package to **Azure Artifacts**.

```
- task: Maven@3

  inputs:

    mavenPomFile: 'pom.xml'

    goals: 'deploy'

    options: '-Drevision=1.1.0'  # Specify the new
version here
```

This ensures that the package version **1.1.0** is published to the Azure Artifacts feed.

In projects that consume this package, ensure that the **pom.xml** or **csproj** files are updated to the correct version:

```
<dependency>

  <groupId>com.yourcompany</groupId>

  <artifactId>your-shared-library</artifactId>
```

```
  <version>1.1.0</version>

</dependency>
```

If a new version causes issues, you can modify the version back to the previous stable release in both the package's configuration and the consuming projects. Once rolled back, commit the changes and the pipeline will ensure that the previous version is restored. The ability to upgrade, downgrade, or roll back versions as needed provides a safeguard against potential issues, allowing for smoother releases and safer rollouts.

Publishing Artifacts from Build Pipelines

Our next task now is to **publish the NuGet package artifacts** created during the build process so that new versions of the application can be distributed through **Azure Artifacts**.

Leveraging the Existing Build Pipeline

You've already built a **NuGet-based project**, where the build process creates **NuGet packages**. The CI/CD pipeline we previously established is responsible for building the project and restoring dependencies using **NuGet**.

The next step involves:

- Building the project and generating the **NuGet package (.nupkg)**.
- Automatically publishing the generated NuGet package to **Azure Artifacts**, making it available for other projects, environments, or teams to consume.

Modifying the Pipeline to Publish NuGet Artifacts

We will modify the **azure-pipelines.yml** file to include steps for **publishing the NuGet package** to Azure Artifacts.

Given below is how the YAML file should look, updated to include steps for packing and publishing the **NuGet** package:

```
trigger:

  - master



pool:
```

```
  vmImage: 'windows-latest'

steps:
  # Restore NuGet packages
  - task: NuGetCommand@2
    inputs:
      command: 'restore'
      feedsToUse: 'select'
      vstsFeed: 'yourorganization/SpringBootNuGetFeed'

  # Build the project and create a NuGet package
  - task: NuGetCommand@2
    inputs:
      command: 'pack'
      packagesToPack: '**/*.csproj'
      versioningScheme: 'byBuildNumber'
      includeReferencedProjects: true

  # Push the NuGet package to Azure Artifacts
  - task: NuGetCommand@2
    inputs:
```

```
      command: 'push'

      packagesToPush:
'$(Build.ArtifactStagingDirectory)/*.nupkg'

      nuGetFeedType: 'internal'

      publishVstsFeed:
'yourorganization/SpringBootNuGetFeed'
```

In the above YAML,

- **NuGetCommand@2 - restore**: Restores the NuGet packages needed by the project, fetching them from the **SpringBootNuGetFeed** in Azure Artifacts.
- **NuGetCommand@2 - pack**: This task builds and packages the project, creating a **.nupkg** file that will later be published.
- The **packagesToPack** input specifies the **.csproj** file or files to package.
- The **versioningScheme** ensures the package versions are controlled by the build number or another versioning scheme.
- **NuGetCommand@2 - push**: This step publishes the created NuGet package to the **Azure Artifacts** feed, making it available for use in other projects or environments.

Accessing and Using Published NuGet Packages

Once the NuGet packages are published, they are available in **Azure Artifacts** for distribution and reuse as follows:

- After a successful pipeline run, navigate to **Azure DevOps > Artifacts**.
- In the **SpringBootNuGetFeed** feed, you will find the newly published package along with its version number.
- To use the published package in another project, add the package as a dependency in the **packages.config** or **csproj** file.

A quick example:

```
<PackageReference Include="Your.Shared.Library"
Version="1.0.0" />
```

If a subsequent pipeline stage or another project needs to consume this package, you can configure **NuGet restore** to pull the latest version from Azure Artifacts:

```
steps:

- task: NuGetCommand@2

  inputs:

    command: 'restore'

    feedsToUse: 'select'

    vstsFeed: 'yourorganization/SpringBootNuGetFeed'
```

Managing Versions of Published Artifacts

In case the latest version causes issues, you can easily roll back to a previous version by specifying the required version in the project's **csproj** or **packages.config** file.

```
<PackageReference Include="Your.Shared.Library"
Version="1.0.0" />
```

Once your package is published and available, it can be used in **continuous deployment** pipelines or other CI processes. Whether you are deploying new versions of a service or using the package in other projects, all this automation makes it easy to manage version control, updates, and rollbacks efficiently.

Summary

In conclusion, our main takeaways included the use of Azure Artifacts for version control and dependency management within our CI/CD flows. We learned how to set up Azure Artifacts to store and share packages like Maven and NuGet between projects, ensuring that dependencies are centrally managed and easily accessible. Our Spring Boot project was able to incorporate Maven and NuGet packages after we set up these feeds, automating the process of pulling the correct dependencies during each build.

The chapter then discussed how to handle version control for these packages. We maintained stability across builds by specifying exact versions in the pom.xml or csproj files for Maven and NuGet, respectively. We also learned how to upgrade and roll back to previous versions in case newer versions caused problems. At last, we showed you how to upload build artifacts to Azure

Artifacts. This included both Spring Boot JAR files and Maven/NuGet package management. With this automated artifact management system in place, all project dependencies can be stored in one place, and the development and deployment processes can be made more efficient.

Chapter 6: Testing and Quality Assurance with Azure Test Plans

Overview

Azure Test Plans is a comprehensive tool that enables teams to plan, track, and execute manual and automated tests, ensuring that software meets quality expectations. This chapter will focus on using Azure Test Plans to implement effective testing and quality assurance processes in your project. The chapter will walk you through the initial configuration of Azure Test Plans and how to use them for manual testing of your applications, allowing teams to create structured test cases and track results directly within Azure DevOps.

You will also learn how to automate test cases with Postman and integrate them into your CI/CD pipeline. We will look at how to set up Postman collections and run them through the pipeline to test API behavior and application performance. Furthermore, the chapter discusses integrating test results into Azure Pipelines, which ensures that all test case results, whether manual or automated, can be tracked in one place. Finally, you will learn about exploratory testing, a technique that allows testers to run tests dynamically and adapt to potential issues as they arise, providing a versatile approach to discovering bugs and edge cases in the application.

Up and Running with Azure Test Plans

In this chapter, we will build upon the work we've completed so far in setting up a robust **CI/CD pipeline** for our Spring Boot application, managing dependencies through **Azure Artifacts**, and integrating automated testing using tools like **JUnit** and **Mockito**. Now, the focus shifts to **Azure Test Plans**, a key feature of **Azure DevOps** designed to support manual and automated testing processes.

To begin working with **Azure Test Plans**, we first need to set it up in our existing Azure DevOps environment.

Activating Azure Test Plans

Azure Test Plans is a built-in service within Azure DevOps but may not be enabled by default in your project. Given below is how to get it up and running:

- Navigate to your Azure DevOps organization and select the **project** where you want to configure Azure Test Plans.
- From the left-hand sidebar, select **Test Plans**. If you don't see the **Test Plans** option, you may need to add the **Azure Test Plans** service to your project.
- Azure Test Plans may require activation as a paid service, depending on your Azure DevOps plan. If Test Plans is not included in your subscription, you can activate it by navigating to **Azure DevOps Organization Settings > Billing**, and purchasing **Test Plans** for your team.

The basic features for manual testing may be available with the free tier, but advanced features, such as automated test execution, may require a license.

Configuring Azure Test Plans

Once Azure Test Plans is activated, the next step is configuring it for your specific project's testing requirements.

Create a Test Plan

- Click on **New Test Plan** to create a new plan where your team will organize test cases.
- Give the test plan a descriptive name (e.g., **Spring Boot Application Tests**) and associate it with the current iteration or sprint to track progress against specific development milestones.

Define Test Suites

Test Suites group related test cases under a single category. Create suites like **Functional Testing**, **API Testing**, or **UI Testing** to organize different types of tests. For example, you may have a suite specifically for testing the Spring Boot application's API functionality.

You can set up different test suites for manual testing, exploratory testing, and automated test cases.

Adding Team Members

Ensure that relevant team members, such as developers and QA engineers, are added to the project and have permissions to access and manage test plans. You can manage permissions by going to **Project Settings > Security > Test Plans** and configuring roles accordingly.

Integrating with Work Items

Link test cases to **work items** such as user stories or bugs. This will allow the team to track the test coverage of user stories and ensure that each story or bug has corresponding test cases.

Configuring Azure Test Runner for Manual Tests

Azure Test Runner is a feature within Azure Test Plans that allows testers to run manual tests directly in the browser while tracking results and capturing information such as screenshots, videos, and comments during test execution.

- Go to the **Test Plans** tab, select a test case, and click on **Run** to start testing using the built-in **Test Runner**.
- As you go through the test steps, you can pass or fail each one and provide detailed feedback for developers to address any issues.

- The results will automatically be captured in Azure DevOps, giving the team real-time visibility into the status of each test case.

After this configuration, your project will have a fully integrated testing environment in Azure Test Plans. With this configuration, your testing processes are optimized and seamlessly integrated into the larger Azure DevOps pipeline, whether you are running manual tests, associating test cases with tasks, or getting ready for automated testing.

Setting up Test Plans for Manual Testing

Manual testing is important for verifying features that require human input, such as UI components or workflows that cannot be easily automated. In this section, we will focus on creating and managing **manual test cases** in **Azure Test Plans**. We will walk through how to create structured test cases, execute them, and track the results directly.

Creating Structured Test Cases

A **test case** in Azure Test Plans is a set of predefined steps, data, and expected results that help validate whether a feature or functionality works as intended. Given below is how to create manual test cases:

- In Azure DevOps, open the project where you want to create test cases.
- Select **Test Plans** from the left menu.
- If you haven't already created a test plan, click **New Test Plan**, name it (e.g., **Spring Boot Functional Tests**), and associate it with a specific iteration or sprint if applicable.
- Test plans allow you to organize different sets of test cases within a single framework.
- Inside the test plan, you can create **Test Suites**, which are collections of related test cases. Test suites can be based on criteria like functional areas (e.g., login functionality, API endpoints) or specific user stories.
- Click **New** to add a **Requirement-based Suite** or **Static Suite**, depending on whether you want to base your tests on specific work items or just organize them manually.
- Within a test suite, click **New Test Case** to create a structured test case. A test case consists of multiple parts, including **title**, **steps**, **expected results**, and **parameters**.
- Enter a **Title** that clearly describes the test (e.g., "Test user login with valid credentials").
- Add individual test **steps** under **Action** that describe what needs to be done. Each step should be clear and concise, such as:
    - Navigate to the login page.

    - Enter a valid username.
    - Enter a valid password.
    - Click the login button.
- In the **Expected Result** field, specify the outcome for each step. For example:
- After clicking the login button, the user should be redirected to the dashboard.

Then, click **Save and Close** to save the test case to the selected suite.

Executing Manual Tests

Once the test cases are created, the next step is to execute them and track the results as below:

- In the **Test Plans** tab, select the test plan and the suite you want to execute.
- Click on **Run** to begin executing the test cases manually.
- Azure Test Plans offers an in-built tool called **Test Runner** for executing manual tests.
- Test Runner will load each test step sequentially. For each step, the tester can pass or fail the test and provide comments or additional details if needed.
    - **Pass** or **Fail** each step as you proceed.
    - **Capture screenshots**, add **comments**, or even record a video to provide detailed feedback to developers.
    - If a bug is encountered, you can create a **Bug** work item directly from the Test Runner interface and link it to the test case.
- As you complete each test case, you can mark the overall test case as **Passed**, **Failed**, or **Blocked** (if you encounter an issue preventing you from continuing).

Once all the above steps are completed, **Save** the results.

Tracking and Reviewing Test Results

After running the manual tests, you can review the results directly in Azure DevOps. Following are the steps to track the progress:

- Navigate back to the **Test Plans** page to see the results of your executed test cases.
- The test cases will show their current status: **Passed**, **Failed**, or **Not Run**.
- If test cases are linked to work items (like user stories or bugs), you can view how these test results impact the overall progress of a specific work item.

- Click on a specific test case to drill down into the detailed results, including execution history, tester comments, and any bugs that were filed during testing.

Azure DevOps allows you to generate reports and visualize testing progress. These reports help you analyze test coverage, track how many test cases passed or failed, and understand where bottlenecks in the development cycle might exist.

Automating Test Cases with Postman

Postman is a powerful tool used for testing RESTful APIs, allowing us to send requests, receive responses, and validate outputs. It also supports test automation through **collections**, which can be integrated directly into the CI/CD pipeline for continuous testing.

In this section, we will learn how to use **Postman** to automate API test cases that we manually tested earlier. We will cover how to install and configure Postman in our environment, create **Postman collections** for testing, and then automate those tests in Azure Pipelines.

Installing and Configuring Postman

Installing Postman

- Go to the Postman website and download the appropriate version for your operating system.
- Install the application and launch it.
- Create an account or log in to your existing Postman account.
- Postman will display the main workspace where you can start creating requests and collections for testing.

Configuring Postman for Spring Boot Application

Within Postman,

- click **New > Collection** to create a collection that will store your API requests.
- Name the collection (e.g., **Spring Boot API Tests**).
- This collection will hold all API endpoints you want to test (e.g., login, user management, etc.).
- Click **Add Request** within the collection to add your first API request.

For example, if you want to test the login functionality, configure the request as follows:

```
Method: POST
```

URL: `http://localhost:8080/api/login (replace with the actual API endpoint).`

In the **Body** tab, specify the credentials for the login request:

```
{
  "username": "testuser",
  "password": "password123"
}
```

After configuring the request, switch to the **Tests** tab to add assertions that will validate the API response. Postman uses **JavaScript** for writing test cases.

For example, to check if the status code is **200** for a successful login:

```
pm.test("Login successful", function () {
  pm.response.to.have.status(200);
});
```

You can add additional tests, such as validating the response body, headers, or specific fields. And then, **Save the Request** to the collection.

Automating Test Cases with Postman in CI/CD Pipeline

Exporting the Postman Collection

To run the Postman tests in the CI/CD pipeline, you need to export the collection:

- Click on the collection name, then select **Export**.
- Save the collection as a **JSON file** (e.g., **SpringBootAPITests.json**) to a directory in your project or repository.

Newman is Postman's command-line tool for running collections. It's used to automate the execution of Postman tests in CI/CD environments. You can install Newman globally on your local machine or CI environment:

```
npm install -g newman
```

Adding the Collection to Pipeline

Now that we have the Postman collection exported and Newman installed, we will configure our Azure DevOps pipeline to run the API tests during the build process.

- Upload the **Postman collection JSON file** (SpringBootAPITests.json) to your repository.
- Add a new step to the **CI/CD pipeline** to run the Postman tests using Newman:

```
trigger:

  - master


pool:

  vmImage: 'ubuntu-latest'


steps:

# Restore dependencies and build your project (existing
steps)


# Install Newman

- script: |

    npm install -g newman

  displayName: 'Install Newman'


# Run Postman Collection with Newman
```

```
- script: |
    newman run SpringBootAPITests.json --reporters cli,junit --reporter-junit-export results/TEST-postman-results.xml
  displayName: 'Run API tests with Postman'

# Publish test results
- task: PublishTestResults@2
  inputs:
    testResultsFormat: 'JUnit'
    testResultsFiles: 'results/TEST-postman-results.xml'
    failTaskOnFailedTests: true
```

Executing Automated Postman Tests in Pipeline

After adding the steps for Postman automation in your pipeline, commit the changes and push them to the repository. The CI/CD pipeline will now automatically:

- Build the project.
- Run the Postman API tests using Newman.
- Generate and publish test results to Azure DevOps.

Viewing Test Results in Azure DevOps

Once the pipeline completes, you can view the test results in Azure DevOps as below:

- Go to **Pipelines > Runs** in Azure DevOps and open the latest pipeline run.
- In the pipeline summary, you will find a section for **Test Results**. You can see the outcome of the Postman tests, including passed and failed tests.
- For each failed test, detailed logs are available, helping you debug issues.

Overall, automating the API tests in the pipeline ensures that every build is validated against the expected API behavior, significantly improving the reliability of the application. The test results are automatically published in Azure DevOps for the team to review the success or failure of each API test case easily.

Integrating Test Results into Azure Pipelines

In this section, we will focus on **integrating test results** from both **manual test cases** and **automated test cases** into **Azure Pipelines**, so that all test outcomes can be tracked in one place.

Viewing Manual Test Results in Azure Pipelines

Manual Test Cases in Azure Test Plans

Manual test cases are run directly from **Azure Test Plans** using the **Test Runner** tool. Once these test cases are executed, the results are stored in Azure Test Plans, but they can also be integrated into Azure Pipelines so that test results from different stages are aggregated.

Follow the steps:

- Go to **Test Plans** in Azure DevOps and execute the manual test cases.
- During execution, the tester will pass or fail steps, add comments, and create bug work items if needed.
- After running the manual tests, their results are available in the **Test Plans** section, but they can also be linked to the work items (like user stories) or build pipelines for tracking progress.
- Then, go to Pipelines > Runs.
- Select the appropriate pipeline run, and navigate to the **Tests** tab.
- You will see manual test results alongside automated ones, making it easy to track both types of tests in one location.

Linking Manual Tests to Work Items and Build Pipelines

To ensure that manual test results are integrated into Azure Pipelines, you can:

- Link manual test cases to work items (e.g., user stories or bugs).
- As test cases are executed and marked pass/fail, their results will be reflected in the linked work items and can be tracked through **Build Pipelines** as well.

Viewing Automated Test Results in Azure Pipelines

Automated Test Cases with Postman

In the previous section, we set up **Postman** collections and executed the tests automatically using **Newman** in the CI/CD pipeline. These automated tests can generate results in **JUnit** format, which Azure Pipelines can consume and display.

When the pipeline runs, the automated tests are executed, and the results are saved as **JUnit** reports.

These test results are published as part of the pipeline using the **PublishTestResults** task. We then can configure the following task in the **azure-pipelines.yml** file to publish test results:

```
- task: PublishTestResults@2
  inputs:
    testResultsFormat: 'JUnit'
    testResultsFiles: 'results/TEST-postman-results.xml'
    failTaskOnFailedTests: true
```

This task reads the test result file generated by Newman or any other testing tool and publishes it to Azure Pipelines.

Viewing Automated Test Results in Azure Pipelines

Once the pipeline finishes executing the automated tests:

- Go to **Pipelines > Runs** and select the run you want to inspect.
- In the **Summary** tab, there will be a **Tests** section showing the overall results of all tests executed in the pipeline.
- You can view specific test logs and any errors or assertions that caused tests to fail.

You can also monitor the overall progress and health of your application by tracking the pass/fail rates of both manual and automated tests in one place. The **Test Runs** tab in **Azure Pipelines** provides a dashboard-style view, showing statistics for both manual and automated tests over time, helping you spot trends and areas that require attention.

By integrating both manual and automated tests in Azure Pipelines, you have a centralized view of the application's quality and can respond quickly to any issues detected during the testing process.

Perform Exploratory Testing

Exploratory testing is a dynamic and unscripted approach to software testing that focuses on exploring the functionality and behavior of an application without predefined test cases. The goal is to uncover hidden bugs, edge cases, and usability issues by actively interacting with the application in creative and intuitive ways. Unlike structured testing, where every action is predefined, exploratory testing allows testers to think freely, act on intuition, and respond to real-time observations to identify potential defects in the software. This makes it especially useful when dealing with complex workflows or scenarios that cannot be easily automated or fully covered by manual test cases.

Purpose of Exploratory Testing

The key purpose of exploratory testing:

- Traditional testing often focuses on predefined functionality, but exploratory testing aims to discover bugs that may be hidden in untested areas of the application.
- By testing the application in a fluid manner, exploratory testing mimics how real users might interact with the software, making it easier to spot usability or functional issues.
- It allows testers to quickly assess the stability of a new feature or system before moving to more structured testing.
- Testers can use their experience and creativity to explore areas that might otherwise be overlooked in structured test plans.

Configuring Azure Test Plans for Exploratory Testing

In **Azure Test Plans**, exploratory testing is supported via the **Exploratory Testing** feature, which helps teams capture bugs, comments, screenshots, and other data during ad-hoc testing sessions.

Following are the steps you can configure and run exploratory testing:

- Install the **Azure Test Plans Extension** for your browser (available for Chrome and Edge).
- This extension allows you to run exploratory testing sessions directly from your browser, capturing interactions, bugs, and feedback along the way.
- In Azure DevOps, navigate to **Test Plans**.
- From the left sidebar, select **Exploratory Testing**.

- Click on **New session**, where you can specify the **work item** or **user story** that you want to explore. This step links the session to a specific feature or bug, providing better traceability.

Once the session is started, the extension will open in a new tab, ready to track your interactions with the application.

Performing Exploratory Testing

We will perform an exploratory test on a key feature, such as the **login functionality** of the Spring Boot application. The idea is to use the application as a real user might, exploring various paths that may not have been covered by earlier tests.

To do this:

- Use the application (hosted locally or on a server) by visiting the login page (e.g., **http://localhost:8080/api/login**).
- Perform typical user actions, such as entering valid credentials, invalid credentials, or leaving fields empty to see how the system responds.

As you navigate through the application, the **Azure Test Plans extension** captures screenshots, logs actions, and allows you to write notes. For example, you might test invalid login scenarios (e.g., incorrect password or username) to see if the application correctly handles errors.

When you spot an unexpected behavior (e.g., the login page freezes when invalid credentials are entered), you can log this as a **bug**.

- To file a bug, click **Create Bug** within the browser extension.
- The tool automatically attaches relevant information (e.g., screenshots, the sequence of actions, browser details) to the bug, making it easier for developers to reproduce and fix the issue.
- Try logging in with special characters or SQL injection attempts in the username field.
- Try refreshing the page during form submission or logging in with extremely long strings.

Once you've explored the feature thoroughly, you can end the session by clicking **End Session** in the browser extension. The results are automatically saved in Azure Test Plans, along with any bugs, screenshots, or notes taken during the session.

Reviewing Test Results and Bugs

Once the exploratory session is complete, you can review all the bugs and findings in **Azure DevOps** as below:

- In **Azure Test Plans**, go to the **Exploratory Testing** section and select your session.

- You will see a summary of all actions performed, along with any bugs or issues that were logged during the session.
- Each bug is linked to the session, making it easier to trace the bug back to the specific exploratory session where it was found.

Developers can view the detailed steps that led to the bug, along with any relevant screenshots or recordings, which simplifies debugging and fixing.

The overall flexibility of exploratory testing, combined with the detailed logging features of Azure DevOps, makes it an invaluable tool for improving software quality, especially when dealing with dynamic or complex features.

Summary

Shortly put, we used Azure Test Plans to perform different aspects of testing and quality assurance. To start, we integrated Azure Test Plans into our preexisting DevOps infrastructure to provide a framework for managing and organizing our manual and automated tests. After setting up manual test cases and making structured test plans with clear procedures and outcomes in mind, the next step was to run the tests in Azure Test Runner and monitor the progress.

Next, we focused on automating test cases for API testing with Postman, creating Postman collections for our Spring Boot application. These collections were added to the CI/CD pipeline via Newman, allowing for continuous testing and validation of our API endpoints. The automated test results were captured and published to Azure Pipelines alongside the manual test results, resulting in a more comprehensive view of test outcomes.

We then looked into integrating all test results, both manual and automated, into Azure Pipelines, which would provide us with a centralized location to track the application's quality and progress. Finally, we looked at exploratory testing, which involved running unscripted, dynamic testing sessions to find unexpected bugs or issues with the application. Problems discovered during these sessions were recorded and monitored in Azure DevOps, which gave useful information that might have been missed by more strict, predetermined tests.

CHAPTER 7: INFRASTRUCTURE AUTOMATION WITH AZURE PIPELINES

Overview

In this chapter, we will learn how to use current IaC tools and practices to automate the process of providing, deploying, and managing the infrastructure for a Spring Boot application. The chapter begins by discussing Terraform to define and automate infrastructure resources in a declarative manner. You will learn how to use Terraform and Azure Pipelines to manage infrastructure.

Following this, we go into the process of preparing the necessary infrastructure for deploying the Spring Boot application, including virtual machines, networking components, and storage. After that, you will learn how to containerize the application with Docker and deploy it to AKS, ensuring scalability and efficient resource management. We will also go over how to perform database migrations with Flyway, a tool that simplifies database version control. You will learn how to automate schema migrations within the CI/CD pipeline, ensuring that your application and database evolve in sync.

Finally, the chapter will cover configuring disaster recovery in Azure Pipelines, showing how to automate failover and backup processes to ensure your application's resilience and availability in the event of an infrastructure failure. You will come out of this chapter with an extensive understanding of how to use Azure Pipelines to automate your infrastructure management and application deployment processes.

Up and Running with Terraform and IaC

In this section, we introduce **Terraform**, a widely-used **IaC** tool, which allows us to define, provision, and manage cloud infrastructure in a consistent and automated manner. Terraform uses a declarative language to describe the infrastructure resources you need, and then it takes care of provisioning those resources in the specified cloud environment, in this case, **Microsoft Azure**. Using **Azure Pipelines** to integrate Terraform into your CI/CD workflow ensures that infrastructure is treated as code, allowing for version control, collaboration, and automation across teams.

Installing and Configuring Terraform in Azure

Installing Terraform

To begin, we first need to install Terraform. And, you can install Terraform on your local machine or use it directly in Azure Pipelines. To do this,

- Visit the official Terraform website to download the Terraform CLI for your operating system.
- Follow the installation instructions for your specific OS (Windows, macOS, or Linux).

- Once installed, verify that Terraform is installed correctly by running the following command in your terminal:

```
terraform -version
```

You should see the installed Terraform version displayed.

Configuring Terraform with Azure

Before using Terraform to manage Azure infrastructure, you need to authenticate Terraform to work with your Azure subscription.

- Install Azure CLI

If not already installed, download and install the **Azure CLI** from the Microsoft website.

- Authenticate Azure CLI

Once installed, log in to your Azure account via the CLI:

```
az login
```

This opens a browser window for you to log in. After successful authentication, the CLI will return a list of subscriptions associated with your Azure account.

- Configure Service Principal for Terraform

Terraform requires a **Service Principal** to interact with Azure. You can create one using the Azure CLI:

```
az ad sp create-for-rbac --role="Contributor" --
scopes="/subscriptions/{subscription-id}"
```

Save the output of this command, which includes **appId**, **password**, and **tenant** ID, as you will need these credentials for Terraform to authenticate.

Writing Terraform Code to Manage App Infrastructure

Now, we will define the infrastructure required to deploy the **Spring Boot application** in Azure using Terraform. This will typically include resources like a **Virtual Network**, **Azure App Service**, **Azure SQL Database** (or another database service), and storage.

To do this, we will create a file named **main.tf** in your project repository. This file will contain the Terraform code for defining infrastructure.

```
provider "azurerm" {
  features = {}
  subscription_id = "YOUR_AZURE_SUBSCRIPTION_ID"
  client_id       = "YOUR_SERVICE_PRINCIPAL_CLIENT_ID"
  client_secret   = "YOUR_SERVICE_PRINCIPAL_SECRET"
  tenant_id       = "YOUR_TENANT_ID"
}

resource "azurerm_resource_group" "rg" {
  name     = "springboot-rg"
  location = "East US"
}

resource "azurerm_app_service_plan" "appserviceplan" {
  name                = "springboot-appserviceplan"
  location            =
azurerm_resource_group.rg.location
  resource_group_name = azurerm_resource_group.rg.name
  sku {
    tier = "Standard"
    size = "S1"
  }
```

```
}

resource "azurerm_app_service" "appservice" {
  name                = "springboot-app"
  location            =
azurerm_resource_group.rg.location
  resource_group_name = azurerm_resource_group.rg.name
  app_service_plan_id =
azurerm_app_service_plan.appserviceplan.id

  site_config {
    dotnet_framework_version = "v4.0"
  }
}
```

In this Terraform script, we define:

- **Resource Group**: A logical container for managing related resources in Azure.
- **App Service Plan**: Defines the compute resources for hosting your app.
- **App Service**: Hosts the Spring Boot application.

Integrating Terraform into Azure Pipelines

Now that we have a basic Terraform script ready to provision the infrastructure for the Spring Boot application, we will automate the process of running Terraform in **Azure Pipelines**.

To do this,

- In your Azure DevOps project, go to **Pipelines** and click **New Pipeline**.
- Select the repository where the Terraform configuration is stored.

- Choose **YAML** for pipeline configuration.
- Create a **azure-pipelines.yml** file in the root of your repository to automate Terraform actions like **init**, **plan**, and **apply**.

```
trigger:
  - master

pool:
  vmImage: 'ubuntu-latest'

steps:
- task: AzureCLI@2
  inputs:
    azureSubscription: 'Azure Service Connection'
    scriptType: 'bash'
    scriptLocation: 'inlineScript'
    inlineScript: |
      az login --service-principal -u $(clientId) -p
$(clientSecret) --tenant $(tenantId)

- script: |
    terraform init
    terraform plan -out=tfplan
```

```
  displayName: 'Terraform Init and Plan'


- script: |
    terraform apply -auto-approve tfplan
  displayName: 'Terraform Apply'
```

In the Azure DevOps pipeline settings, configure the **clientId**, **clientSecret**, and **tenantId** variables (the service principal details from earlier). This allows the pipeline to authenticate Terraform to your Azure environment.

Then, commit the **azure-pipelines.yml** file to your repository and trigger a pipeline run.

Azure Pipelines will:

- Authenticate to Azure.
- Run **terraform init** to initialize the Terraform workspace.
- Run **terraform plan** to generate a plan for provisioning resources.

Finally, run terraform apply to create the necessary infrastructure in Azure.

With Terraform and Azure Pipelines working together, we can ensure that infrastructure changes are tracked, versioned, and automated, aligning with the principles of **IaC**.

Provisioning Infrastructure for Spring Boot Application

In this section, we will provision the necessary infrastructure to deploy the **Spring Boot application**. We will use **Terraform** and **Azure Pipelines** to automate the process of setting up the required components, including **virtual machines**, **networking components**, and **storage**. These resources will ensure that the application has a secure and scalable environment to run.

Writing Terraform Configuration for the Infrastructure

Here, create a new Terraform configuration file (main.tf) that will define all the resources needed for the infrastructure.

Given below is the sample code for provisioning the necessary resources.

```
provider "azurerm" {
  features = {}
  subscription_id = "YOUR_SUBSCRIPTION_ID"
  client_id       = "YOUR_SERVICE_PRINCIPAL_CLIENT_ID"
  client_secret   = "YOUR_SERVICE_PRINCIPAL_SECRET"
  tenant_id       = "YOUR_TENANT_ID"
}

# Resource Group
resource "azurerm_resource_group" "springboot_rg" {
  name     = "springboot-resource-group"
  location = "East US"
}

# Virtual Network
resource "azurerm_virtual_network" "vnet" {
  name                = "springboot-vnet"
  address_space       = ["10.0.0.0/16"]
  location            =
azurerm_resource_group.springboot_rg.location
  resource_group_name =
azurerm_resource_group.springboot_rg.name
```

```
}

# Subnet
resource "azurerm_subnet" "subnet" {
  name                 = "springboot-subnet"
  resource_group_name  =
azurerm_resource_group.springboot_rg.name
  virtual_network_name =
azurerm_virtual_network.vnet.name
  address_prefixes     = ["10.0.1.0/24"]
}

# Public IP
resource "azurerm_public_ip" "springboot_public_ip" {
  name                = "springboot-public-ip"
  location            =
azurerm_resource_group.springboot_rg.location
  resource_group_name =
azurerm_resource_group.springboot_rg.name
  allocation_method   = "Dynamic"
}
```

```
# Network Security Group (NSG)

resource "azurerm_network_security_group" "nsg" {

  name                = "springboot-nsg"

  location            =
azurerm_resource_group.springboot_rg.location

  resource_group_name =
azurerm_resource_group.springboot_rg.name

}


# NSG Rule (Allow HTTP/HTTPS Traffic)

resource "azurerm_network_security_rule"
"allow_http_https" {

  name                        = "allow-http-https"

  priority                    = 1001

  direction                   = "Inbound"

  access                      = "Allow"

  protocol                    = "Tcp"

  source_port_range           = "*"

  destination_port_ranges     = ["80", "443"]

  source_address_prefix       = "*"

  destination_address_prefix  = "*"

  resource_group_name         =
azurerm_resource_group.springboot_rg.name
```

```
  network_security_group_name =
azurerm_network_security_group.nsg.name
}


# Network Interface
resource "azurerm_network_interface" "springboot_nic" {
  name                = "springboot-nic"
  location            =
azurerm_resource_group.springboot_rg.location
  resource_group_name =
azurerm_resource_group.springboot_rg.name


  ip_configuration {
    name                          = "internal"
    subnet_id                     =
azurerm_subnet.subnet.id
    private_ip_address_allocation = "Dynamic"
    public_ip_address_id          =
azurerm_public_ip.springboot_public_ip.id
  }
}


# Virtual Machine
```

```
resource "azurerm_virtual_machine" "vm" {
  name                  = "springboot-vm"
  location              =
azurerm_resource_group.springboot_rg.location
  resource_group_name   =
azurerm_resource_group.springboot_rg.name
  network_interface_ids =
[azurerm_network_interface.springboot_nic.id]
  vm_size               = "Standard_DS1_v2"

  # OS Disk Configuration
  storage_os_disk {
    name              = "osdisk"
    caching           = "ReadWrite"
    create_option     = "FromImage"
    managed_disk_type = "Standard_LRS"
  }

  # OS Configuration
  os_profile {
    computer_name  = "springboot-vm"
    admin_username = "azureuser"
```

```
    admin_password = "P@ssword1234!"
  }

  # Linux VM
  os_profile_linux_config {
    disable_password_authentication = false
  }

  # Image Reference
  storage_image_reference {
    publisher = "Canonical"
    offer     = "UbuntuServer"
    sku       = "18.04-LTS"
    version   = "latest"
  }
}

# Storage Account
resource "azurerm_storage_account" "springboot_storage" {
  name                     = "springbootstorage"
  resource_group_name      =
azurerm_resource_group.springboot_rg.name
```

```
  location                    =
azurerm_resource_group.springboot_rg.location

  account_tier                = "Standard"

  account_replication_type    = "LRS"

}
```

This configuration creates a **Virtual Network** (VNet) with a subnet, a **Virtual Machine (VM)** running Ubuntu, a **Network Security Group (NSG)** to manage traffic, a **public IP** for external access, and a **storage account** to store data or logs.

Integrating Terraform with Azure Pipelines

Now that we've defined our infrastructure, the next step is to automate its provisioning using **Azure Pipelines**. For this, add the following to the **azure-pipelines.yml** file to automate the deployment of the defined infrastructure using **Terraform**.

```
trigger:

  - master


pool:

  vmImage: 'ubuntu-latest'


steps:

  # Install Terraform

  - task: TerraformInstaller@0

    inputs:

      terraformVersion: 'latest'
```

```
  # Azure CLI Login
  - task: AzureCLI@2
    inputs:
      azureSubscription: 'Azure Service Connection'
      scriptType: 'bash'
      scriptLocation: 'inlineScript'
      inlineScript: |
        az login --service-principal -u $(clientId) -p
$(clientSecret) --tenant $(tenantId)

  # Terraform Init
  - script: |
      terraform init
    displayName: 'Terraform Init'

  # Terraform Plan
  - script: |
      terraform plan -out=tfplan
    displayName: 'Terraform Plan'
```

```
# Terraform Apply

- script: |

    terraform apply -auto-approve tfplan

  displayName: 'Terraform Apply'
```

Then, in the **Azure DevOps pipeline settings**, configure the **clientId**, **clientSecret**, **tenantId**, and **subscriptionId** environment variables for the service principal authentication.

After committing the **azure-pipelines.yml** file to your repository, trigger a pipeline run as shown below:

```
Initialize Terraform (terraform init).

Generate a plan for the resources (terraform plan).
```

Verifying Infrastructure in Azure

Once the pipeline completes successfully, you can verify the infrastructure:

- Check the **Azure Portal** under **Networking** for the virtual network (VNet) and its subnet.
- Look under Compute > Virtual Machines to see the provisioned VM.
- Verify the creation of the storage account under **Storage Accounts**.
- Check the **Network Security Group** for the rules controlling traffic to your virtual machine.

Deploying Spring Boot to the Provisioned VM

Now that the infrastructure is ready, you can SSH into the VM and deploy the application. This can be done as below:

- Retrieve the public IP of the VM and SSH into it:

```
ssh azureuser@<public_ip>
```

- On the VM, install **Java** if it's not installed:

```
sudo apt update
```

```
sudo apt install openjdk-11-jre
```

- Copy the **Spring Boot JAR** file to the VM using SCP or by downloading it directly from your source repository:

```
scp path/to/springboot-app.jar
azureuser@<public_ip>:/home/azureuser
```

- Start the Spring Boot application:

```
java -jar springboot-app.jar
```

Your Spring Boot application is now running on the provisioned infrastructure!

By leveraging **Terraform** to **Azure Pipelines**, we established a robust, automated process for provisioning cloud resources, enabling the deployment of the application with minimal manual intervention.

Containerize and Deploy Application to AKS

Containerization ensures that the application runs in a consistent environment, regardless of where it is deployed. **AKS**, which is Microsoft Azure's Kubernetes service, provides an orchestration platform that can manage containers at scale. In this section, we will **containerize** the app using **Docker** and then deploy it to **AKS**.

Install and Configure Docker

Docker is a platform that simplifies the development, shipping, and running of applications inside containers. Before we containerize our application, we need to download and install **Docker Desktop** from the official Docker website.

And then, after installation, ensure Docker is running by checking the status in your terminal:

```
docker --version
```

Then, create a Dockerfile. For your knowledge, a **Dockerfile** is a script that contains a series of commands to assemble an image for your application.

In the root of the application, create a **Dockerfile** with the following content:

```
# Use an official OpenJDK runtime as a parent image
FROM openjdk:11-jre-slim

# Set the working directory inside the container
WORKDIR /app

# Copy the Spring Boot JAR file into the container
COPY target/springboot-app.jar /app/springboot-app.jar

# Run the Spring Boot application
ENTRYPOINT ["java", "-jar", "springboot-app.jar"]
```

This **Dockerfile** specifies that the image will use **OpenJDK 11** as the base image, copy the built JAR file from the **target** directory to the container, and set the entry point to run the JAR file.

Once the **Dockerfile** is ready, build the Docker image using the following command:

```
docker build -t springboot-app .
```

This command builds the image from the **Dockerfile** and tags it as **springboot-app**.

Now, to test the container locally before deploying it to Kubernetes, run the following command:

```
docker run -p 8080:8080 springboot-app
```

The Spring Boot application should now be accessible on **localhost:8080**.

Introduction to AKS

AKS is a managed Kubernetes service that simplifies the deployment, management, and operations of Kubernetes clusters. It provides features like automated scaling, monitoring, and integrated security. AKS allows you to run containers at scale and ensures that applications remain resilient and available.

Provision an AKS Cluster

Create a Resource Group

Before creating the AKS cluster, we need a resource group to hold all the associated resources:

```
az group create --name springboot-aks-rg --location
eastus
```

Create an AKS Cluster

Create an AKS cluster with one node pool. The following command provisions the AKS cluster in the resource group we just created:

```
az aks create --resource-group springboot-aks-rg --name
springboot-aks-cluster --node-count 1 --enable-addons
monitoring --generate-ssh-keys
```

Connect to the AKS Cluster

Once the cluster is created, configure **kubectl** (the Kubernetes CLI tool) to connect to the AKS cluster:

```
az aks get-credentials --resource-group springboot-aks-rg
--name springboot-aks-cluster
```

This command sets up the kubeconfig file to communicate with the AKS cluster.

Pushing Docker Image to Azure Container Registry

ACR allows you to store and manage container images in Azure. To deploy the Docker container to Kubernetes, we first need to push the Docker image to **Azure Container Registry (ACR)** as below:

- Create an ACR instance to store the Docker image.

```
az acr create --resource-group springboot-aks-rg --name
springbootacr --sku Basic
```

- Log in to the container registry to push images.

```
az acr login --name springbootacr
```

- Tag the Docker image with the ACR login server address.

```
docker tag springboot-app
springbootacr.azurecr.io/springboot-app:v1
```

- Push the tagged image to the ACR repository.

```
docker push springbootacr.azurecr.io/springboot-app:v1
```

Deploy Application to AKS

Now that the Docker image is in ACR, we can deploy it to the AKS cluster. In the root of your project, create a file named **deployment.yaml** with the following content:

```
apiVersion: apps/v1

kind: Deployment

metadata:

  name: springboot-deployment

spec:

  replicas: 2

  selector:

    matchLabels:

      app: springboot-app

  template:

    metadata:
```

```yaml
      labels:
        app: springboot-app
    spec:
      containers:
      - name: springboot-app
        image: springbootacr.azurecr.io/springboot-app:v1
        ports:
        - containerPort: 8080
---
apiVersion: v1
kind: Service
metadata:
  name: springboot-service
spec:
  type: LoadBalancer
  ports:
  - port: 80
    targetPort: 8080
  selector:
    app: springboot-app
```

This YAML file creates a **Kubernetes deployment** with two replicas of the Spring Boot container and exposes the application via a **LoadBalancer service** to allow external access.

And then, apply the **deployment.yaml** file to your AKS cluster:

```
kubectl apply -f deployment.yaml
```

Then, check the status of the pods (containers) running on the cluster:

```
kubectl get pods
```

You should see two running pods for the Spring Boot application. And then finally, retrieve the external IP address of the load balancer service:

```
kubectl get service springboot-service
```

Once the external IP is assigned, you can access the Spring Boot application by navigating to the IP address in your browser.

Performing Database Migrations using Flyway

Flyway is a popular open-source tool that allows developers to version and automate database migrations using SQL scripts. This ensures consistency and reliability across development, testing, and production environments, which is crucial when working with cloud platforms like Azure. In this section, we will focus on using **Flyway** to manage database schema changes in a structured, version-controlled manner and then automate the schema migration process within the CI/CD pipeline.

Setting up Flyway

We will configure Flyway to work with an **Azure SQL Database** for our Spring Boot application. If you haven't already set up an **Azure SQL Database**, create one using the Azure CLI as below:

```
az sql server create --name springboot-db-server --
resource-group springboot-aks-rg --location eastus --
admin-user myadmin --admin-password mypassword123!
```

Then, create the database:

```
az sql db create --resource-group springboot-aks-rg --
server springboot-db-server --name springbootdb --
service-objective S0
```

You can then download and install Flyway from the official Flyway website. After installation, ensure Flyway is available by checking the version:

```
flyway -version
```

Flyway uses a **configuration file** to connect to the target database and manage migrations. For this, create a file named **flyway.conf** in the root of your project with the following content:

```
flyway.url=jdbc:sqlserver://springboot-db-
server.database.windows.net:1433;database=springbootdb

flyway.user=myadmin

flyway.password=mypassword123!

flyway.schemas=dbo
```

This configuration connects Flyway to the Azure SQL database using the connection string, username, and password.

Performing a Database Migration

Now that Flyway is installed and configured, we can perform a database migration using SQL scripts. For example, the first migration file should be named V1__initial_schema.sql. These files contain SQL statements that define the changes to the database schema.

Given below is an example of an initial schema script to create a **users** table:

```
CREATE TABLE users (

    id INT PRIMARY KEY IDENTITY(1,1),

    username VARCHAR(50) NOT NULL,

    email VARCHAR(100) NOT NULL,
```

```
    created_at DATETIME DEFAULT GETDATE()
);
```

After saving the SQL file, execute the migration with Flyway:

```
flyway migrate
```

Flyway will look for SQL migration files, apply the changes to the Azure SQL Database, and update the **Flyway metadata table** to track applied migrations.

Once the migration is successful, log into the Azure SQL Database (using tools like **Azure Data Studio** or **SQL Server Management Studio**) and verify that the users table was created.

Also, to view the current state of migrations, you can also run:

```
flyway info
```

Automating Database Migrations in the CI/CD Pipeline

The next step is to automate the database migrations using **Azure Pipelines**.

In your **azure-pipelines.yml** file, add steps to install Flyway and run the migration as part of the build process.

```
trigger:
  - master


pool:
  vmImage: 'ubuntu-latest'


steps:
# Install Flyway
- task: Bash@3
```

```
  inputs:
    targetType: 'inline'
    script: |
      wget -qO-
https://repo1.maven.org/maven2/org/flywaydb/flyway-
commandline/8.0.0/flyway-commandline-8.0.0-linux-
x64.tar.gz | tar xvz
      sudo ln -s `pwd`/flyway-8.0.0/flyway
/usr/local/bin/flyway


# Run Flyway Migration
- task: Bash@3
  inputs:
    targetType: 'inline'
    script: |
      flyway -url=jdbc:sqlserver://springboot-db-
server.database.windows.net:1433;database=springbootdb \
      -user=$(dbUsername) -password=$(dbPassword) migrate
```

In the Azure Pipelines Uconfigure the database credentials as **pipeline variables** (**dbUsername** and **dbPassword**). This allows Flyway to authenticate with the Azure SQL Database.

Once the pipeline is triggered, Flyway will automatically:

- Check for new migration files in the project.
- Apply any pending migrations to the Azure SQL database.

This ensures that any new schema changes are applied as part of the CI/CD pipeline without manual intervention.

In this section, we established and configured **Flyway** in our Azure environment to manage database migrations for the Spring Boot application. Also, we performed an initial migration by creating a **users** table, and then demonstrated how to automate the migration process within the **Azure Pipelines** CI/CD workflow.

Configuring Disaster Recovery in Azure Pipelines

In this section, we will focus on automating **disaster recovery** processes in **Azure Pipelines**, which includes both **failover** and **backup** mechanisms to ensure business continuity. Disaster recovery is critical in cloud environments to maintain application availability in the event of unexpected outages or failures. By automating these processes in Azure Pipelines, we can ensure rapid recovery with minimal downtime.

Disaster Recovery in Azure

In the context of Azure, disaster recovery involves setting up strategies like:

- **Failover**: Automatically switching to a backup or secondary environment in case the primary region experiences an outage.
- **Backup and Restore**: Regularly backing up critical data (databases, file storage, etc.) and ensuring the ability to restore it when needed.

We will automate the following tasks in Azure Pipelines:

- **Automated Backups** of the database and virtual machines.
- **Failover to a Secondary Region** when the primary region is unavailable.

Configuring Automated Backups

Database Backups using Azure SQL Database

Azure SQL Database provides built-in **automated backups** for point-in-time recovery, but we can extend this by creating pipeline jobs to trigger backups manually if needed.

For this, first enable backups for Azure SQL Database:

- To manually trigger a backup in Azure Pipelines, we can create an **Azure CLI task** in the pipeline to initiate an export.
- In the **azure-pipelines.yml** file, add a step to export the database to a storage account as part of the disaster recovery process:

```
trigger:
  - master

pool:
  vmImage: 'ubuntu-latest'

steps:
# Trigger SQL Database Backup
- task: AzureCLI@2
  inputs:
    azureSubscription: 'Azure Service Connection'
    scriptType: 'bash'
    scriptLocation: 'inlineScript'
    inlineScript: |
      az sql db export \
      --admin-password $(dbPassword) \
      --admin-user $(dbUsername) \
      --storage-key $(storageKey) \
      --storage-key-type StorageAccessKey \
      --storage-uri
https://<storage_account>.blob.core.windows.net/backups/s
pringbootdb.bacpac \
```

```
    --name springbootdb \
    --resource-group springboot-aks-rg \
    --server springboot-db-server
```

This script exports the database to a BACPAC file and stores it in an Azure storage account.

Backing up Virtual Machines

If the application is hosted on a **Virtual Machine (VM)**, you can create **VM backups** using **Azure Backup**. Just enable **Azure Backup** on the VM using the Azure Portal or Azure CLI:

```
az backup vault create --resource-group springboot-aks-rg
--name springboot-vault --location eastus

az backup protection enable-for-vm --resource-group
springboot-aks-rg --vault-name springboot-vault --vm
springboot-vm --policy-name DefaultPolicy
```

Add a task to the pipeline to create a backup on-demand:

```
- task: AzureCLI@2
  inputs:
    azureSubscription: 'Azure Service Connection'
    scriptType: 'bash'
    scriptLocation: 'inlineScript'
    inlineScript: |
      az backup protection backup-now --resource-group
springboot-aks-rg \
      --vault-name springboot-vault --container-name
springboot-vm \
```

```
    --item-name springboot-vm --retain-until 30-12-2024
```

This command triggers an immediate VM backup and retains it until the specified date.

Automating Failover to a Secondary Region

Setting up Azure SQL Failover Groups

Failover Groups in Azure allow you to automatically failover the database to a secondary region in case the primary region goes down.

Now, let us setup a **failover group** for the Azure SQL Database across two regions:

```
az sql failover-group create \
--name springboot-failover-group \
--partner-server springboot-db-server-secondary \
--resource-group springboot-aks-rg \
--server springboot-db-server \
--failover-policy Automatic
```

This will ensure that if the primary server goes down, the secondary server will take over automatically.

Add the following task to automate a failover in case of an issue in the primary region:

```
- task: AzureCLI@2
  inputs:
    azureSubscription: 'Azure Service Connection'
    scriptType: 'bash'
    scriptLocation: 'inlineScript'
    inlineScript: |
```

```
      az sql failover-group set-primary \
      --name springboot-failover-group \
      --resource-group springboot-aks-rg \
      --server springboot-db-server-secondary
```

This command forces a failover to the secondary region.

Configuring Virtual Machine Failover

For **VM failover**, we can leverage **Azure Site Recovery** (ASR), which automates VM failover between regions.

You can do this by setting up **Azure Site Recovery** to replicate your VM to a secondary region:

```
az site-recovery replication-vault create --name springboot-recovery-vault --resource-group springboot-aks-rg --location eastus

az site-recovery protection-container create --vault-name springboot-recovery-vault --name springboot-vm-container --resource-group springboot-aks-rg
```

Add a task in the pipeline to trigger VM failover:

```
- task: AzureCLI@2
  inputs:
    azureSubscription: 'Azure Service Connection'
    scriptType: 'bash'
    scriptLocation: 'inlineScript'
    inlineScript: |
      az site-recovery failover begin \
```

```
--resource-group springboot-aks-rg \
--vault-name springboot-recovery-vault \
--replicated-item-name springboot-vm \
--failover-direction PrimaryToSecondary
```

Once you have set up automated backups and failover mechanisms, you test these processes regularly.

In this section, we demonstrated how to configure and automate **disaster recovery** processes in **Azure Pipelines**, focusing on both **automated backups** and **failover** mechanisms. We established automatic backups for **Azure SQL databases** and **Virtual Machines** and set up failover groups for high availability in case of region-level outages.

Summary

In this chapter, we covered how to use Azure Pipelines to automate infrastructure and disaster recovery processes. We began by learning how to use Terraform to define and automate the provisioning of cloud infrastructure for a Spring Boot application, which included configuring virtual machines, networking, and storage. Next, we learned how to containerize the Spring Boot application with Docker and deploy it to AKS. We then used ACR to store the Docker images and Kubernetes deployments to scale the application.

Next, we moved on to Flyway database migrations, where we used the CI/CD pipeline to automate the process of applying schema changes to the Azure SQL Database. Last but not least, we automated backup and failover in Azure as part of our disaster recovery strategy. We ensured seamless failover between regions by configuring automatic failover using Azure SQL Failover Groups and setting up Azure Site Recovery for virtual machines.

CHAPTER 8: COLLABORATION AND TEAM MANAGEMENT IN AZURE DEVOPS

Overview

Now that we've reached the last chapter of this book, we will discover how Azure DevOps improves team management and collaboration, allowing teams to tackle complicated projects more efficiently. The chapter begins with instructions on how to manage work items and create project boards. These features help teams track progress, assign tasks, and manage project workflows in an organized manner. Next, we will look at how to integrate GitHub with Azure DevOps to collaborate seamlessly for version control, CI/CD pipelines and project management.

We will also look at how to set up team workflows in Azure DevOps to automate processes, standardize task management, and ensure that proper procedures are followed during development. Finally, we will go over how to use Azure DevOps Analytics to monitor your project's development to gauge how well your team is doing and how healthy your project is overall. Finally, we will go over how teams can work together on various projects by sharing pipelines and resources, which will make larger projects run more smoothly and improve collaboration.

Managing Work Items and Project Boards

In this section, we will explore how to manage **work items** and set up **project boards** in **Azure Boards**. Azure Boards provides powerful tools for tracking work items, managing sprints, and visualizing project progress. Work items can include tasks, bugs, user stories, and more, and they are essential for organizing and planning your team's workflow.

Managing Work Items

Work items in Azure Boards represent units of work that need to be completed, such as tasks, user stories, bugs, or features.

Given below are the steps to manage them:

- Navigate to your Azure DevOps project.
- In the left menu, select **Boards > Work Items**.
- To create a new work item, click the **New Work Item** button and choose the type of work item you want to create, such as **Task**, **Bug**, or **User Story**.
- Fill in the details, such as **Title**, **Assigned To**, **Priority**, and **Iteration Path** (which links it to a sprint or project milestone).
- Click **Save & Close** to add the work item.

You can update existing work items by selecting them from the **Work Items** page and modifying the fields. Changes can include updating the status, adding comments, or assigning the item to a different team member.

Work items can be tracked using queries. Create a query to view work items based on criteria like assigned user, status, or iteration. These queries help teams prioritize and manage work effectively.

Work items can be linked to other items, such as linking a **Bug** to a **User Story** or a **Task** to a **Feature**. This allows teams to see dependencies and relationships between different parts of the project.

Setting up Project Boards

Project boards in Azure Boards provide a visual way to track the progress of work items across different stages of the workflow (e.g., **To Do**, **In Progress**, **Done**). Given below are the steps to set up project boards:

Accessing Project Boards

In the Azure DevOps project, select **Boards** from the left navigation pane, and then click on **Boards** to view the project board.

Project boards have default columns like **To Do**, **In Progress**, and **Done**, but you can customize them based on your team's workflow. To do this,

- Click on the **Column Options** button in the top-right corner of the board and select **Column Settings**.
- Add, rename, or remove columns to fit your workflow. For instance, you can add columns like **Testing** or **Review**.

Adding Work Items to the Board

Drag and drop existing work items onto the board, or create new work items directly from the board by clicking **+ New Item** under the appropriate column.

Assign items to team members by opening the work item and selecting the **Assigned To** field.

As work progresses, team members can move items across the board by dragging and dropping them from one column to another (e.g., moving a task from **In Progress** to **Done**).

Using Swimlanes for Organization

Swimlanes allow further categorization of work items on the board. You can set up swimlanes based on priority, team assignments, or work item types.

To configure swimlanes, go to **Column Options > Swimlanes** and add categories based on your team's needs.

Managing Sprints and Iterations

Azure Boards also allows teams to manage **sprints** and iterations, which are used to organize work items over a defined period.

Defining Sprints

Navigate to **Boards > Sprints**, and create new iterations for the project by clicking **New Child** under the project's **Iterations** section.

Assign work items to specific sprints by dragging and dropping them into the sprint backlog.

Tracking Sprint Progress

Use the **Sprint Backlog** view to track work completed during each sprint. It includes details like burndown charts, work remaining, and work completed to help teams stay on track.

Through work items, project boards, and sprints, teams are empowered to plan, execute, and track their projects with greater clarity and alignment.

Integrating GitHub with Azure DevOps

In this section, we will focus on **integrating GitHub with Azure DevOps** to enable seamless collaboration and version control between the two platforms. By connecting GitHub repositories with Azure DevOps, you can automate your CI/CD pipelines, manage code updates, and track the entire project lifecycle efficiently. This integration ensures that any changes made in the GitHub repository can automatically trigger pipeline builds in Azure DevOps, maintaining synchronization between development and deployment processes.

Connecting GitHub Repositories to Azure DevOps

Linking GitHub to Azure DevOps Project

- Navigate to Azure Pipelines
  - Open your Azure DevOps project and go to **Pipelines > Pipelines** in the left menu.
  - Click on **New Pipeline** to create a new pipeline.
- Choose GitHub as the Repository Source
  - In the next step, you will be asked to choose the code repository location. Select **GitHub**.
  - If you haven't connected your GitHub account to Azure DevOps yet, click on **Authorize**. This will redirect you to GitHub for authorization. Log in with your GitHub credentials and authorize Azure DevOps to access your repositories.

- Select Your GitHub Repository
    - Once authorization is complete, Azure DevOps will display a list of repositories linked to your GitHub account.
    - Select the repository that contains your Spring Boot application or any other relevant project for which you want to configure CI/CD.

Setting up Version Control with GitHub and Azure DevOps

Configuring a Build Pipeline

- Define the Build Pipeline

After selecting your GitHub repository, Azure DevOps will automatically suggest a pipeline template based on your project type (e.g., **Java with Maven** for Spring Boot).

Choose the template, or select **Starter Pipeline** if you want to configure it manually.

- Configure YAML for Version Control

Azure DevOps uses a **YAML file** to define CI/CD pipeline configurations. The pipeline file can be stored directly in your GitHub repository under .github/workflows or in the repository root under .azure-pipelines.yml.

Given below is an example of a simple **YAML** pipeline that triggers builds based on changes in the repository:

```
trigger:

  - master

pool:

  vmImage: 'ubuntu-latest'


steps:

- script: |

    echo "Starting build process"

    mvn clean install
```

```
  displayName: 'Build Spring Boot Application'
```

This configuration defines that the pipeline should trigger every time there's a push or pull request to the **master** branch in the GitHub repository.

- Commit the Pipeline

After defining your pipeline in the YAML file, commit it to your GitHub repository. Azure DevOps will automatically detect this and display the pipeline in the Pipelines dashboard.

Enabling Version Control for CI/CD Pipelines

- Automatic Trigger for Builds

Once the pipeline is configured, every time you push a commit or create a pull request in GitHub, the pipeline will be triggered automatically. Azure DevOps will pull the latest code from GitHub, build the project, and perform the defined steps (e.g., running tests, packaging the application).

In the **Pipeline > Runs** section of Azure DevOps, you can track the status of each build and view logs for debugging if something goes wrong.

- Branching and Version Control Strategy

To set up version control effectively, create different pipelines for various branches such as **development**, **staging**, and **production**.

For instance, you can define a pipeline that only triggers on changes to the **production** branch:

```
trigger:
  branches:
    include:
      - production
```

This ensures that only approved changes reach the production environment, following version control best practices.

Configuring GitHub Pull Requests with Azure DevOps

You can configure GitHub **Pull Requests (PRs)** to automatically trigger build and test workflows in Azure DevOps.

- Enable PR Triggers

In the YAML pipeline file, you can configure a trigger that runs the CI pipeline whenever a pull request is made:

```
pr:

  branches:

    include:

      - '*'
```

This setup ensures that any pull request made to any branch will trigger the pipeline, allowing you to verify that the proposed changes won't break the build before they are merged into the main branch.

- View CI Results in GitHub

Once the pipeline is linked with GitHub, the build results for every PR will be visible directly in GitHub under the **Checks** tab. This visibility provides immediate feedback to developers, helping them ensure that their changes are functional and adhere to the codebase quality standards.

Monitoring and Managing Pipelines in Azure DevOps

- View Pipeline Runs

In Azure DevOps, navigate to **Pipelines > Runs** to see all recent pipeline runs triggered by GitHub commits or pull requests. For each run, you can view details such as build duration, test results, and logs.

- Troubleshooting and Debugging

If a pipeline run fails, Azure DevOps provides detailed logs that help in identifying issues. Use these logs to troubleshoot problems in the build or deployment process.

- Setting up Notifications

You can configure **notifications** in Azure DevOps to alert your team when a build or deployment fails. These alerts can be sent via email, Slack, or other communication tools integrated with Azure DevOps.

This integration simplifies the management of your repositories, pipelines, and team workflows, ensuring that every code change triggers automated builds, tests, and deployments. Through the use of GitHub **pull requests** and **branching strategies**, you can maintain a robust version control system while automating the process with Azure Pipelines.

Setting up Team Workflows

In this section, we will focus on setting up **team workflows** in **Azure DevOps**. Workflows ensure that teams follow standardized procedures, automate common processes, and streamline task management, ultimately improving team efficiency. With Azure DevOps, you can automate various aspects of your development cycle, from code reviews to deployments, ensuring that tasks are completed consistently across the team.

Setting up Team Workflows in Azure DevOps

Setting up standardized workflows in Azure DevOps provides several benefits:

- Every team member follows the same process for work items, pull requests, and code reviews.
- With clear workflows, developers, testers, and project managers know the exact status of tasks, reducing confusion and enhancing team communication.
- Automated tasks, such as running tests or triggering deployments, reduce manual effort, allowing teams to focus on higher-priority tasks.
- With workflows in place, tasks are automatically assigned and tracked, making it easier to manage responsibilities within the team.

Workflows in Azure DevOps can involve a combination of task management, automated testing, build triggers, approvals, and more.

Given below are the steps to set up and manage team workflows:

Define Your Workflow Processes

Work items (such as **user stories**, **tasks**, or **bugs**) follow a lifecycle that can be customized according to your team's needs. Azure Boards provides default work item states like **New**, **In Progress**, and **Done**.

You can customize this lifecycle to fit your team's workflow. For instance, you may want to add states such as **Testing** or **Review**.

To do this, navigate to **Boards > Process** in Azure DevOps and select the process type for your project (Agile, Scrum, or Basic). Customize work item states by adding new states or changing transitions between states. This helps ensure that work items follow a standardized process.

For example, when a developer completes a task, it can automatically transition to **In Review**, indicating the need for peer review before further progress.

Define Approval and Code Review Workflow

- Setup Pull Request Approvals

Within **Repositories > Branches**, configure branch policies to require **code reviews** before changes are merged into the main branch.

Set a policy to require at least one or more reviewers for any **pull request** made to a specific branch.

Additionally, you can require that pull requests pass **automated build checks** and have zero **merge conflicts** before they are allowed to be merged.

- Automating Workflows with Pipelines

Use Azure Pipelines to automate tasks like **unit tests**, **builds**, and **deployments** as part of the workflow. These tasks can be triggered automatically when a pull request is created or updated.

Define specific conditions in your pipeline's YAML file to trigger different stages of your CI/CD process based on the workflow. For example, a successful build can automatically trigger a deployment to a staging environment.

Automating Processes with Workflows

Use **Azure Pipelines** to set up an automated testing workflow. Whenever a developer pushes code to a feature branch or creates a pull request, the pipeline can automatically run **unit tests, integration tests**, or **end-to-end tests**.

For example, add a step in the pipeline to run automated tests before merging a pull request:

```
steps:

- task: Maven@3

  inputs:

    mavenPomFile: 'pom.xml'

    goals: 'test'
```

The results of these tests can then be automatically reported back to the pull request in GitHub or Azure Repos, informing the team whether the code is stable.

You can automate **release pipelines** to ensure that deployments happen consistently and reliably. For this, set up the workflows where after successful builds and tests, code is automatically promoted from **development** to **staging** or **production** environments. And, add gates and approvals to these releases for added control.

```
stages:
```

```
- stage: Staging
  jobs:
  - job: DeployToStaging
    steps:
    - script: echo "Deploying to staging"
```

These workflows help standardize processes, reducing ambiguity and improving team productivity. Through automation, workflows ensure that critical processes like testing, code reviews, and deployments happen consistently, making collaboration more seamless and task management more effective.

Tracking Project Progress with Azure DevOps Analytics

In this section, we will focus on **tracking project progress** and using **Azure DevOps Analytics** to gain insights into team performance and project health. Azure DevOps provides built-in dashboards, reports, and analytics views to help project managers and teams understand how the project is progressing and make data-driven decisions.

Accessing Azure DevOps Analytics

Azure DevOps comes with **Analytics Views** and dashboards that provide data about work items, builds, releases, test results, and other critical metrics. Following are the steps to access these insights:

- In your Azure DevOps project, go to **Overview > Dashboards**. From here, you can either create a new dashboard or view existing ones.
- Azure DevOps also has a **built-in Analytics widget** that can be added to dashboards to display key performance indicators.
- In the left menu, select **Boards > Reports**. Azure DevOps includes several pre-built reports that focus on work items, sprint burndowns, velocity, and more. These reports give a quick overview of how the project is performing.
- You can extend the reporting capabilities by installing the **Azure DevOps Analytics Marketplace extension**. This adds more detailed insights and advanced visualization tools.

Tracking Project Progress using Dashboards and Widgets

Dashboards in Azure DevOps are customizable and allow you to display various widgets that track project metrics. You can create dashboards for different teams, areas, or iterations of the project.

Setting up a Dashboard

- Go to Overview > Dashboards and click New Dashboard.
- Name the dashboard based on the focus, such as **Sprint Overview** or **Team Progress**.
- Add widgets that provide critical metrics such as **Work Progress**, **Burndown charts**, and **Velocity**.

Key Widgets to Track Project Progress

- Work Items

Displays the number of work items (e.g., tasks, user stories, bugs) that are currently open, in progress, or completed.

- Sprint Burndown

Shows how much work remains in the current sprint and how much has been completed. This helps track if the team is on pace to complete the work by the sprint's end.

- Velocity Chart

Displays the team's velocity across previous sprints, helping to predict how much work can be completed in future sprints.

- Work Breakdown

Provides a visual breakdown of the work items assigned to each team member, showing how much work is in progress and completed.

Tracking Builds and Releases

You can add build and release widgets to track the health of CI/CD pipelines. For example:

- **Build Success/Failure**: Displays the status of recent builds, including successes, failures, and duration.
- **Release Pipeline Progress**: Shows the status of ongoing releases and the percentage of successful deployments.

Insights into Team Performance

Using Velocity and Capacity Reports

- The **Velocity Report** in Azure DevOps shows how much work the team has completed in previous sprints, measured in story points or tasks completed. This helps in understanding team performance over time.
- The **Capacity Report** shows how much work each team member has been allocated and how much of that capacity has been utilized, helping balance workloads.

Sprint Analytics

Go to **Boards > Sprints**, and from here, you can view **Sprint Analytics**, which shows the team's progress in the current sprint. The analytics view shows how much work has been completed, what's left, and whether the team is on track to meet sprint goals.

Cycle Time and Lead Time

- **Cycle Time** measures how long it takes for work to move from "In Progress" to "Done," helping teams optimize the development process.
- **Lead Time** tracks how long it takes for work to move from creation to completion. These metrics help teams identify bottlenecks in their workflow.

Custom Reports for Project Health

Creating Custom Queries

Use **Queries** to generate custom reports that track project health. For example, you can create a query that tracks all work items by state, priority, or assigned team member.

Go to **Boards > Queries** and create a new query based on your needs. For instance, you can create a query to show all tasks in a sprint that are still open and assigned to a specific team member.

Work Item Analytics

With **Work Item Analytics**, you can generate insights into how efficiently tasks are being completed. This includes tracking the **average time in progress**, **task completion rates**, and identifying work items that are consistently delayed.

Exporting Data to Power BI

For deeper insights, Azure DevOps allows you to export data to **Power BI**, Microsoft's advanced data visualization tool. This enables teams to create customized dashboards and reports with more advanced analytics and trend analysis.

These analytics help ensure that projects stay on track and that teams remain productive, aligned, and efficient.

Collaborating across Teams with Shared Pipelines and Projects

In this section, we will focus on **collaborating across teams using shared pipelines and projects** in **Azure DevOps**. Collaboration between multiple teams working on different projects is crucial in complex environments, where code bases, infrastructure, and workflows often overlap.

Understanding Shared Pipelines and Resources

Shared pipelines allow multiple teams to use the same CI/CD pipelines for building, testing, and deploying their projects, even if they are working on different repositories or environments. By centralizing pipelines, teams benefit from consistent processes and avoid redundant configurations.

Common resources such as libraries, tools, and infrastructure (like databases or cloud environments) can also be shared between projects. This setup promotes collaboration and consistency while reducing administrative overhead.

Setting up Shared Pipelines

Using Multi-Project Pipelines

Azure DevOps enables the creation of **multi-project pipelines**, where multiple teams or projects can use the same pipeline definition. This is particularly useful for teams working on interrelated projects, such as microservices, where each service might have its own repository but relies on a shared pipeline for deployment.

- Define a Shared Pipeline in YAML

Start by defining a common pipeline template in YAML that can be referenced by different teams. This template could include tasks like building, testing, and deploying.

Save the pipeline template in a shared repository that all teams have access to. For example:

```
# templates/build-and-deploy.yml

steps:

- task: Maven@3
```

```yaml
  inputs:
    mavenPomFile: 'pom.xml'
    goals: 'clean install'
- task: PublishBuildArtifacts@1
  inputs:
    artifactName: 'drop'
```

- Reference the Shared Pipeline in Different Projects

In the YAML pipelines of individual projects, you can reference the shared pipeline template:

```yaml
trigger:
  branches:
    include:
      - master


pool:
  vmImage: 'ubuntu-latest'


resources:
  repositories:
    - repository: sharedPipelines
      type: git
      name: shared/pipelines
```

```
steps:

- template: build-and-deploy.yml@sharedPipelines
```

This approach ensures that all projects use the same build and deploy process, making it easy to enforce standard practices across teams.

Cross-Project Pipeline Triggers

Cross-project pipeline triggers allow teams to set up workflows where a build or release pipeline in one project triggers a pipeline in another project. This is useful in scenarios where different teams are working on interdependent components.

- Create a Trigger

In the YAML configuration of the downstream project, use the **resources** keyword to define a trigger based on the pipeline from another project:

```
resources:

  pipelines:

    - pipeline: sharedPipeline

      project: sharedProject

      source: 'ci-pipeline'

      trigger:

        branches:

          include:

            - master
```

This configuration ensures that whenever the **shared pipeline** in the **shared project** is triggered, it will automatically trigger the pipeline in the downstream project as well. This is ideal for coordinating releases across multiple services or teams.

In addition to pipelines, teams can share common resources such as artifacts, environments, and libraries across different projects.

Sharing Artifacts Between Projects

Azure DevOps supports sharing build artifacts between projects using the **PublishBuildArtifacts** and **DownloadBuildArtifacts** tasks.

- Publishing Artifacts

In the upstream project, publish the build artifacts to a shared location:

```
steps:
- task: PublishBuildArtifacts@1
  inputs:
    artifactName: 'drop'
    targetPath: '$(Build.ArtifactStagingDirectory)/drop'
```

- Consuming Artifacts

In the downstream project, reference and download the shared artifact:

```
steps:
- task: DownloadBuildArtifacts@0
  inputs:
    buildType: 'specific'
    project: 'sharedProject'
    buildVersionToDownload: 'latest'
    artifactName: 'drop'
```

This approach ensures that the downstream project uses the latest version of the artifact built by another project, enabling teams to collaborate more efficiently.

Sharing Azure Resources

If multiple teams need access to shared **Azure resources** (e.g., databases, storage accounts, or Kubernetes clusters), you can set up shared infrastructure in Azure that is accessed by multiple projects.

- Using ARM Templates

Set up shared infrastructure using **ARM templates** stored in a central repository. These templates can be referenced by multiple teams to provision and manage the shared resources:

```
steps:
- task: AzureResourceGroupDeployment@2
  inputs:
    azureSubscription: 'AzureServiceConnection'
    resourceGroupName: 'sharedResourceGroup'
    location: 'East US'
    templateLocation: 'Linked artifact'
    csmFile: 'templates/shared-infrastructure.json'
```

- Managing Shared Environments

Multiple teams can deploy to the same **AKS** cluster or **Azure App Service** environment by referencing the shared resources in their deployment pipelines. This helps ensure that infrastructure costs are optimized and resources are used consistently across the organization.

By setting up multi-project pipelines, using cross-project triggers, and sharing build artifacts and Azure infrastructure, teams can reduce duplication, enhance collaboration, and accelerate their delivery processes. With shared pipelines, teams follow the same practices, which ensures smooth coordination between different projects for better alignment and successful project outcomes.

Summary

To summarize what we learned in our final chapter, first, we looked at how to manage work items and create project boards in Azure Boards including organizing tasks, tracking progress, and visualizing workflows more efficiently. After that, we went over the steps to connect GitHub to Azure DevOps to automate builds and tests whenever changes were pushed to GitHub. We learned how to automate code reviews, pull requests, and deployment approvals.

Finally, we looked into Azure DevOps Analytics, which showed us how far along we were in the project, how well our teams were doing, and how healthy our sprints were. We also looked at how teams could collaborate on shared pipelines and resources across multiple projects, resulting in better coordination and efficiency. Teams were able to streamline their development workflows across the organization, improve collaboration, and reduce redundancy by sharing infrastructure, artifacts, and pipelines.

Index

Epilogue

Our progress in "Learning Azure DevOps" has been remarkable, and I am proud of all of us as we near the finish line. Starting with the first project setup and progressing through automated CI/CD pipelines, containerized deployments, and infrastructure automation, it has been a fulfilling experience guiding you through the layers of Azure DevOps. The goal of this book was not only to teach you the tools, but also to inspire you to think critically and apply the DevOps mindset to real-world problems. I hope you are now confident in using the platform to streamline workflows and improve team collaboration.

One of the main points I wanted to make throughout this book was how important automation and standardization are in today's cloud environments. Every chapter, whether it was about pipeline creation, test automation, or infrastructure as code, aimed to lay a solid foundation for automating repetitive tasks and creating consistent, repeatable processes. Now that you know how much work and time Azure DevOps can help you save, I hope you can see how these practices can be integrated into your development lifecycle.

Productivity on an individual level isn't everything in modern DevOps; what matters is how well teams collaborate to produce high-quality software promptly. You've seen how Azure DevOps breaks down silos with shared pipelines, Azure Boards, and GitHub integration, resulting in increased transparency and alignment across roles. I hope you've recognized how these tools can help your teams become more collaborative and productive. The skills and principles you've learned here, such as the value of automated testing, infrastructure resilience, and cross-team collaboration, will continue to serve you well. The hands-on experience you've received will equip you to remain flexible and responsive when confronted with rapid change, whether you're supervising a small team or guiding intricate multi-cloud projects.

Please don't stop exploring, learning, and adjusting these practices to match the specific requirements of your teams and projects. DevOps is not a destination, but rather a continuous journey motivated by a desire to improve processes, embrace automation, and deliver value faster and more consistently.

Keep building, automating, and innovating!

Thank You

www.ingramcontent.com/pod-product-compliance
Lightning Source LLC
Chambersburg PA
CBHW080213170726
48282CB00030B/1098
* 9 7 8 8 1 1 9 1 7 7 3 1 8 *